BECOMING A

Friend & Lover

BECOMING A

Friend & Lover

DICK PURNELL

Here's Life
Publishers

P.O. Box 1576, San Bernardino, CA 92402

Published by
HERE'S LIFE PUBLISHERS, INC.
P.O. Box 1576
San Bernardino, CA 92402

Library of Congress Cataloging-in-Publication Data

Purnell, Dick.
    Becoming a friend and lover.

    Bibliography: p.
    1. Friendship.   2. Intimacy (Psychology)   I. Title.
BJ1533.F8P87   1986   158'.2   85-27018
ISBN 0-89840-107-0 (pbk.)

HLP Product No. 951186

FOR MORE INFORMATION, WRITE:

L.I.F.E. — P.O. Box A399, Sydney South 2000, Australia
Campus Crusade for Christ of Canada — Box 300, Vancouver, B.C., V6C 2X3, Canada
Campus Crusade for Christ — 103 Friar Street, Reading RG1 1EP, Berkshire, England
Lay Institute for Evangelism — P.O. Box 8786, Auckland 3, New Zealand
Great Commission Movement of Nigeria — P.O. Box 500, Jos, Plateau State Nigeria, West Africa
Life Ministry — P.O. Box/Bus 91015, Auckland Park 2006, Republic of South Africa
Campus Crusade for Christ International — Arrowhead Springs, San Bernardino, CA 92414, U.S.A.

To Paula

My Best Friend and Lover

CONTENTS

FOREWORD

We see many books today written on the concerns of married life. Few are being written on the concerns of living a biblical adult lifestyle before marriage. Fewer still present the ups and downs, the frustrations and satisfactions, the defeats and victories of learning to relate with others, while seeking or wondering about a marriage partner, as does this book.

In our clinic, we see many single adults asking the same questions about relating with others, including dating partners and potential mates, that Dick Purnell answers here soundly and in great detail. Amid his answers, single adults will find intriguing, real-life examples (sometimes all too reminiscent of their own) that illustrate Dick's positive advice as to how to relate and view both single and married life.

Dick's openness in presenting the ups and downs of his own years of living singly, as well as his experiences in guiding other singles in attempts to build loving, lasting relationships, make this book all the more important. Few people can speak from such wide experience in both these areas.

Dick stresses the importance of building a friendship with a person to whom you are attracted, and then he tells you how to accomplish that and how not to accomplish it. Becoming a friend of the one you love or hope to love is of paramount importance. If a marriage relationship is to be strong, a mate should, first of all, become one's closest friend.

With today's emphasis all around us on having sexual relationships with anyone whenever it feels good, singles who seek to live a biblically-oriented life are left with much confusion and many temptations. Those few who struggle to save sex for marriage sometimes get married primarily to satisfy growing sexual desires, in order to have society accept them as a completed (i.e., sexually active) man or woman, or for other insufficient and thoroughly wrong reasons.

Singles who desire marriage for these wrong reasons may need a therapist to help them view correctly their single life and the seeking of a mate. Should they go ahead and take the plunge, marrying for any of these wrong reasons, they are likely to need therapy all the more. They then will find themselves unsuccessfully striving to change a relationship built on an unstable foundation into one that fulfills what Dick calls the five-pointed star of an intimate relationship — the social, mental, emotional, spiritual, and physical. Reading this book could be a first and major step for singles desiring to marry for wrong reasons to begin to view aright the relationships, opportunities and outlook that God meant singlehood to afford.

As Dick has observed, relating with someone of the opposite sex often becomes harder over the years instead of easier, because of unhealed emotional wounds and unforgiven bitterness. Each new relationship or potential for a relationship is entered into more cautiously and more of oneself is held back. Learning not only to forgive and to forget but also how to build friendship first is explained in great detail, with illustrations along the way, with which many single adults can identify.

He shows the importance of knowing and understanding how a potential mate thinks in all five areas of life before considering marrying that person. He also gives the problems that develop if any one of the five areas is overemphasized in a relationship, to the neglect of others. A balanced relationship is what works best and Dick presents solid ways to achieve such balance.

He also stresses that before marriage is the time to build the qualities that will make for a good married life, qualities which also help in living a successful single life. Marriage has been called God's way of showing what love is through the interaction of two people who know Him. Single life, also, is a way of learning to see and know God's love, often through a broader spectrum of people than through marriage. This is because a married person's time for interaction with those outside his or her immediate family often is more limited.

Dick's open attitude regarding his own learning experiences in relating with others, as a single, is refreshing and will benefit those who think they are among a very few who struggle for happiness and success in life as a single adult. His ideas are both biblically and psychologically sound.

If more single adults would realize that their lifestyle offers unique opportunities for learning more about befriending other people, we psychiatrists and therapists would have a lot fewer unstable marriages to help put back together.

Paul Meier, M. D.

ACKNOWLEDGMENTS

For more than fifteen months this book has been in the process of coming into being. It has been a long, adventuresome road. I believe the concepts and suggestions I have expressed will help many people become better friends and better lovers.

Those who assisted me in bringing this book into existence did so with hard work, deep thinking and much prayer.

Paula Purnell encouraged me to keep working, sacrificed personal desires, critiqued my writing and hung in there with me.

Marty Williams Anderson generated ideas, wrote the final form of the manuscript and kept me on target.

Carol Douglass researched material, wrote some sections and motivated me to keep going.

Barb Lane offered suggestions and helped stylize the manuscript.

Tina Hood typed my dictation, arranged my speaking schedule and handled a thousand details.

Curt Anderson coordinated the speaking ministry and supervised the office functions while I studied and wrote.

David Blackard handled hundreds of details for Paula, Rachel and me on my speaking trips so I could take time to write.

Angela Bellomy edited the "Time Out with Dick Purnell" publication, handled the ministry ledgers and worked on the word processor so I could be free to write this book.

Chapter One
The Search for a Lasting Love

Mark, a friend of mine, dates a lot. Many of the women he goes with are charming, outgoing and friendly. He admits that it's been fun dating so many women over the years, but it's been frustrating as well.

"All I want, really," Mark tells me, "is to be special in one woman's life."

After numerous traumatic and broken relationships, Mark is still looking for that one person to fulfill his life.

"As a single," Mark says, "relationships between the sexes remind me of entering contests. You yearn for one of the prizes dangled as bait to get you to enter the contest. Yet, once you do, you never win. You enter more and more contests, thinking surely you'll win next time. But the prize is never yours. You begin to feel that the chances of finding a love that lasts a lifetime are as negligible as the chances of winning a contest with thousands of contestants and only one prize!"

Like Mark, if you're an adult, not married and not even dating someone seriously, it's hard to feel fulfilled. I know. I was single until the age of forty-two. Married people constantly told me that I needed to get married and settle down in order to find fulfillment in my life. Yet, when I looked at the married people around me and their problems, I knew that marriage didn't automatically bring lasting satisfaction. It took something more than a wedding to do that.

So, for years, I tried to ignore all the good-hearted encouragement to marry. During that time, I dated many women, but I was so involved in my work that I didn't feel an overwhelming desire to marry and face the potential of trading one set of problems for another. Although my work gave me great satisfaction and I saw no immediate reason for marrying, I did sense a desire to open my life to someone. I wanted to find out what another person was like and for that person to know what I was like. But did I dare open myself to another person and risk my future happiness?

In my late twenties, I began to experience deep struggles and frustrations about being single. There were times when I would open my heart to a woman but if the relationship didn't go anywhere or broke down, I felt betrayed. I had given out deep knowledge of myself but the other person had walked away from it, not wanting to know more of me. At times, I was afraid that I might never find someone to love and that no one would ever love me.

Like me, many single adults want to develop an intimate relationship that won't fail or break up. With almost half of the marriages ending in divorce, they don't want to become a part of that statistic. Some singles, after having tried and failed, sense a deep insecurity even to the point of feeling completely incapable of developing a deep relationship.

You approach someone with little attempts at conversation. Instead of responding, the other person picks up on your remarks as an excuse to voice his or her own concerns. Two people merely talking without communicating their hearts. That becomes a good definition of "boring"! Words without a heart. You turn away, thinking, "Oh, what's the use?" and that's that. Superficial conversations at parties, work, and church leave you empty.

Sometimes you just sit at home alone, feeling unloved and unlovable, convinced that you are incapable of any type of significant relationship. Maybe you even go through the "pity party" syndrome, and you sing, "Woe is me. Nobody loves me. Everybody hates me. Guess I'll go eat worms!"

Recently I counseled a girl named Gwen several times about her longings for an intimate relationship with a man. While on a trip, she wrote to me, saying, "Unless I'm dating a man seriously, I don't feel much like a person. Oh, I know my parents and friends love me, but I want something much deeper. I see my friends walking arm in arm with their lovers, but all I can do is appreciate such intimacy from a distance. I'm never able to feel that closeness and joy, that electrifying oneness. I need a sense of hope and courage that someday I'll have that, too."

Losing at Lasting Love

Some singles live with a lack of hope, a refusal to believe that anyone would love them for a lifetime. Others fear being unable to love anyone else for a lifetime!

After speaking at Washington State University, a girl said, "You spoke about commitment and that I should eventually be committed to someone in marriage for a lifetime. But what is commitment? I have a hard time committing myself to someone for even one date! Whenever I'm on a date, I keep looking around at other men and become dissatisfied with the one I'm dating."

Often, singles project their past or present failures or fickleness into the future. They think, *I've had other relationships that have failed. I guess my future relationships will fail, too.* So, although they have a desire to relate intimately with someone, they give up. They no longer try.

While counseling students at Indiana University, a doctor asked me to speak to Marsha, a young woman who was being treated for depression. When I entered Marsha's hospital room, she was buried under the bedcovers. She didn't acknowledge my presence even though she was awake. I tried to start a conversation, but she only responded indirectly. I asked numerous questions but got few answers.

Finally, I said, "Marsha, could it be that you don't want to relate to me because you feel like you have nothing worth saying, because you feel like a failure?"

"Well, yes," she replied.

Encouraged by this small response, I asked, "Have you ever tried to start a relationship and failed?"

"Oh, yes," she said, "often."

"Do you look down on yourself?" I continued, "Do you have a hard time thinking that people care about you?"

Her reply was a revealing, "Yes, so why should I try to start a relationship? It will only fail, end and hurt."

Romance Is Not the Living End

Obviously, most people don't go to Marsha's extreme, but many give up on finding lasting satisfaction in relationships. They desperately want intimacy but don't know how to get it. Other singles have given up on relationships except for an idealistic, romantic look toward marriage for all their satisfaction and fulfillment. They have read or heard that romantic and sexual love is the total answer, yet fail to experience the fulfillment available to them in other kinds of relationships, whether as a married or single person. They think that if there is romance in their lives, they will be happy. Then the lights will go on. Only then. But one person, a marriage partner, can't fill all our needs and never was meant to.

Putting a major emphasis on romance and sexual involvement is often a cover-up for hurt and inability to get close to someone mentally and emotionally. Sometimes those who seek fulfillment only in romance and marriage have had painful relationships in the past:

Just when needed, a close friend had to leave or didn't seem to understand.

A secret shared with a friend was passed on to others and became public knowledge.

An important personal event occurred — graduation or a birthday — and those who meant the most didn't come or even make contact.

A previous marriage turned into a horrible blind alley.

During childhood, a close friend or relative moved or died.

The person had to move away from friends and loved ones himself, perhaps as a child.

Parents were divorced.

In childhood, no one at home seemed to reach out or care.

After experiencing these kinds of losses, a person is less likely to reach out to others, fearful of ever being close to anyone again. In some cases, the person never learns how to have a deep relationship with someone else.

For many years, my friend David was unable to relate with anyone in a caring way. He only wanted to use other people to meet his own needs. He remembers watching television one evening at the age of nine while hearing the familiar sounds of a parental argument in the next room. This time David also heard doors slam. Finally, his father marched through the living room carrying two suitcases.

David ran to his dad, clung to him and tried to pull him back from the door. "No," his dad said, "I've got to go. I refuse to live with your mother any longer."

For years after his dad walked out, David felt only hurt and pain. If his father would leave him, other people would too. In high school and college, David used women for his own selfish desires, never letting anyone get close to his sensitive heart. He never wanted to be rejected again.

A lot of years passed, but finally David began to trust people again, to open himself to others whom he found to be trustworthy. He is learning how to be intimate with others. Now he has hopes of finding that certain someone with whom he can trust his whole self for a lifetime.

Marian, a Christian, was well into middle age before she married. For many years, marriage never seemed personally desirable. Every marriage in her immediate family had been an unhappy one, some ending in divorce. Since childhood, the happiest family member she had known was an unmarried aunt. While Marian had a poor view of marriage, she did have a role model for happy singlehood. So, although friends encouraged her to marry, Marian decided to find happiness as a single person, like her aunt. Determined that she could be both single and fulfilled, she set out to prove it.

Did it work? Yes, until the right person came along. But the right person did not come along until God had shown Marian many happy marriages among her Christian friends. Then she discovered that a fulfilling marriage was not only possible, but possible even for her. She had not been raised to know how to find fulfillment in close relationships. But over her long years of single adulthood, she did learn, through the Lord's guidance, how to relate to and trust friends, relatives and co-workers in ever-deepening friendships for love and satisfaction.

Marian's first priority in intimacy is now her husband, but those other intimate relationships make her marriage all the more fulfilling. They fill up the areas that her marriage relationship wasn't meant to fill. They were the training ground for the deep fulfillment in love and intimacy through being both a friend and lover to her husband, that she has found in marriage.

Loving Others Means Risking Rejection

If love and intimacy are so fulfilling, why do so many married and single people have difficulty finding them? — not just male-female love, but love between close friends of the same sex, love between siblings, love between parents and children? What is so special and yet so fearful about loving people? What is the difference between loving our jobs, loving sports, loving our car, loving a pet, or even loving God, and that kind of love between persons that deeply satisfies our hearts and souls?

The difference is the risk of rejection involved in loving and relating to another person. You don't need to worry about rejection when you love something that is as impersonal as sports or your car. Impersonal things won't turn on you or misunderstand. Only in our imaginations can a love relationship with another person be without risk of rejection and loss.

We Need to Love and Be Loved

When we face reality, we know that love of another person involves risk. Risky love can be one of two basic kinds. C. S. Lewis describes them in his book, *The Four Loves*.[1] One kind is *need-love*, the other *gift-love*. We need the love of others. But we also want to give love to others. Both types of love involve the danger of being rejected. The other person can accept our gift-love but refuse to love us back. In this way, he or she refuses to satisfy our need-love. The other person also can grant us need-love but have such a sense of independence and self-sufficiency that he or she refuses to allow us the satisfaction of gift-love, the giving of love to that person.

We all need to love and accept the love of other people. Even though we talk about being self-sufficient, we are made by God with a need to reach out to others. You can be deeply involved in your job, become successful and go up in your income and status. At the same time, if there is only loveless co-existence between you and others (including the relationship with your mate), the satisfaction you might have from other endeavors is spoiled.

Why do we search for intimacy, for closeness and oneness? Because we want to expose ourselves to someone and to be accepted for just who we are. We are inadequate to rely totally upon ourselves. As Josh McDowell said in *His Image . . . My Image,* "In Christ we are not islands to ourselves. We are all peninsulas in the body of Christ, outgrowths of one another. Our growth as persons depends on our relationships with other people."[2] Intimacy, then, is not only for the purpose of loving and being loved, it also helps us grow and develop as persons.

The Highs and Lows of Desperation

There were times when I desperately yearned for this type of closeness. I was so desirous of getting married that I said, "If I don't find a woman I want to marry by the first of September, I'm going to die." The closer that date came, the higher went my frustration level. Finally, it was August 1, then August 15, and still there was no one on the horizon. September came and went. I didn't die and I didn't find my woman until several years later. Like others, there were times when I felt like I would blow up inside. But I didn't.

As a single person grows older, more of his or her friends drop out of the single world into marriage. This can make a person feel desperate enough to try crazy things.

I came to that point. I was scheduled to speak at The University of Texas. My friend Craig knew a woman I could date for a big event on my day off. He suggested we get three other couples to join us. It sounded great. Before my arrival, I kept calling him, eager to know more about the plans.

When I got there, Craig told me the date was off, but his girl friend Janice, would find me someone else. Immediately I was skeptical. I've always had trouble with blind dates arranged by other women. "She has a great personality," was usually the kindest thing that could be said about them.

My skepticism turned to horror when I discovered that Janice didn't even know my new blind date. A friend of Janice had recommended her. The situation looked bleak indeed. To break the tension, Craig and I joked about what my date might be like, saying, "She probably has two heads or a third eye!"

That night four couples and I piled into a large station wagon and drove to the condominium where my blind date lived. I had everyone line up at her front door, with me standing in the back. That way, while she tried to figure out who I was, I'd check her out and decide what I thought the evening would be like.

When the door opened, there stood a knockout. Anne, a stewardess for United Airlines, was not only good-looking but interesting to talk with.

I'm sure the other guys were jealous of me that night as Anne and I talked and talked. I was thoroughly excited about the evening and showed it. Meanwhile, I thought, *This is it — the first time ever that a blind date has worked out for me!* I asked her for another date, but she was already tied up. Several days later, after my meetings were over, I asked her out again, but she was leaving town on her flight schedule.

On my speaking trip the following month, I ran into Anne at the Atlanta airport. She didn't seem to show much response. Of course, she was busy working at the time, but it took awhile for me to realize that Anne really didn't want to date me again. When it did, all my dreams of dating and developing a relationship with this exciting person had to go out the window. Some dreams die hard.

Like others, I had such a desire for intimacy, that just a glimmer of hope had caused me to pin all my dreams on one meeting. When it didn't work out, I crashed.

Later on, I realized I needed to learn how to develop and sustain intimate relationships for the sake of friendship. Having close friends eases the pain of the search for that special someone of the opposite sex. Then, when that person does come along, we've already learned how to develop a lasting, fulfilling relationship. Since many of our needs will be met through other relationships, we will not expect that special someone to meet more of our needs than one person is capable of doing. Our experience in learning and having intimacy with other friends will make the building of intimacy with that special someone, who is to be our lifetime mate, all the more rewarding.

This book is written to share how to become a friend and lover. It is my hope that you might learn not only to truly love your friends but also to befriend your lover.

1. Why is it difficult to find lasting love?

2. What are you looking for in a relationship with a person of the other sex?

3. What place does romance hold in your love relationships with the other sex?

Chapter Two
The Foundation for Love

As I travel across the country to speak, I have discovered that the primary topic people want to hear about is relationships.

Many of their questions regarding relationships can be summarized in this one question, "How can I become a friend and a lover at the same time?"

We all look for someone to love, both romantically and as an intimate friend. Most of us want to be loved for who we are way down inside and to be able to share our deepest thoughts and feelings with another.

Many people indicate that their first desire is to marry a friend, someone with whom they have enjoyed an intimate companionship, and with whom an emotional relationship has developed. In this way, there will be a strong foundation for a romantic relationship that is not built on superficial ideas or attractions. Many people truly want to be friends first.

Although this is such a widely expressed desire, I have found that the ideal of being a friend first falls victim to the pull of becoming a lover first. Many people know how to be a lover, or are easily swept into that role by their emotions and passions, but they grapple with how to be a friend.

After I spoke on "Sex and the Search for Intimacy" at a southern university, George approached me and said, "I've been dating Diane for several months and we've become very close. In fact, we've made love a couple of times. I really love Diane. But the other day her friends told me she was upset with me. When I phoned her, she said she didn't want to see me again. What's wrong with her?"

"Diane hates you," I replied.

"What do you mean?" George retorted. "I told her I loved her. We made love together. So why does she reject me now?"

Again, I said, "Because she hates you. When you violate a person or overcome their inhibitions with your power, that person may grudgingly participate, perhaps end up even enjoying it at the moment, but later on they will hate you. Just the fact that she told her friends to tell you, instead of telling you herself, shows she doesn't even want to talk with you. She's angry. You became her lover without ever becoming her friend."

In our desire to fill our lives with joy and happiness, we have overlooked the whole idea of friendship. In fact, many of the people we call friends are only acquaintances. Often people have what I call "Hi! Bye!" relationships. They run into someone and say, "Hi, how are you doing?" Then they walk away without waiting for an answer. In fact, they probably don't want an answer. When someone asks you how you're doing, have you noticed how fidgety they get when you actually start to tell them? We live in a sea of superficial relationships.

The Purposes of Dating

Many people have become confused about the purposes of dating. For some, it is a way to have fun and to enjoy carefree activities with a companion. But dating is not just to have fun or to fill your social calendar. You don't date just to find someone who is attractive and with whom you can be romantically or sexually involved.

Primarily, the purpose of dating is to build a relationship with another person. You learn the areas of similarity and differences between yourselves. You learn how to communicate and how to be vulnerable with each other. You also develop common interests and grow in your understanding of the other sex. You learn to encourage and to give to another person. The purpose of dating is not marriage but the development of good, solid relationships. However, dating is the seedbed for marriage either to your current dating partner or to someone yet to come. You form the foundation for a long-term relationship from the first date. The foundation is laid at a time when you don't even know if a relationship will deepen, much less lead to marriage.

When I was on the West Coast speaking at a high school conference, one leader asked to speak with me privately. As we sat in Jerry's car, he related a sequence of short romances. They all followed a pattern. He would meet an attractive woman and quickly begin dating her a lot because of his loneliness and desire for intimacy. Then he would become affectionate while parked in the car or sitting on the living room couch. One thing would lead to another and he would find himself more emotionally infatuated and physically involved than he intended. Then he would end up feeling empty because there was nothing to hold the relationship together except fleeting feelings. That day Jerry asked me, "Why have I done this again? I'm digging myself out of the same hollow situation."

Too often, people start off with physical or romantic activity, hoping that later they will become friends. But the more you become involved physically, the less likely you are to spend quality time talking about deep, significant subjects that really matter to your lives. Physical embracing, which at first may be limited to saying goodbye at the end of a date, ends up becoming the date.

As a result, a couple often find that they have more and more arguments and misunderstandings. Eventually, the relationship deteriorates because it is based on the physical or romantic, rather than on a solid foundation of friendship. After awhile, physical involvement becomes unfulfilling, then, through present pain and memories of past failures, the person cries out, "How can I be different? What can I do?"

My suggestion is to start your relationships differently. Instead of letting your passions and emotions guide the building of a relationship, let your head guide you into a friendship. It may not be easy, but it provides a much better foundation for a healthy and satisfying long-term relationship.

Importance of Friendship

The ability to develop deep friendships determines the depth of emotional intimacy that we will experience in our relationships. McGinnis in *The Friendship Factor* says, "In research at our clinic my colleagues and I have discovered that friendship is the springboard to every other love . . . People with no friends usually have a diminished capacity for sustaining any kind of love."[1] Here he is talking about friends in the real sense, not people you only do things with, but people to whom you can open up your heart and life.

In his article, "The Need for Friendships in Marriage," Dr. Stuart Rosenthal, a professor of psychiatry and a clinical psychiatrist, wrote, "Of the expectations that each partner brings to the marriage itself, three seem to be particularly relevant to friendships: (1) the mate will be loyal, devoted, exclusive; . . . (2) the mate will be a pillar of support in adversity and an ally against the outside world; and (3) the marriage will provide companionship and a hedge against loneliness."[2] In dating, all these aspects are in their rudimentary form. The development of these processes leads to a strong, committed relationship.

Become Friends With Others of Your Own Sex

The ingredients that go into building deep relationships are learned behaviors. Being vulnerable, dealing with conflict and remaining faithful to someone do not come automatically. We learn to be an intimate friend by being involved in intimate friendships.

A great place to start is with a roommate, or a friend who enjoys your same pastimes. You may think these relationships are nothing like a marriage commitment. After all, if you have an argument with a friend, you can just say, "Goodbye, there's the door." In marriage, that isn't so easy. But if you've built no commitment in same-sex relationships, it's hard to develop commitment in other-sex relationships. Commitment is a learned behavior, not an automatic one.

If people have not learned to be vulnerable and to open up their real selves to someone of their own sex, the chances are very high that they will not know how to open up with someone of the opposite sex. Likewise, if people have not learned to be committed in same-sex relationships, they probably won't know how to be committed in other-sex relationships.

Learning to develop strong friendships with members of our own sex presents a perfect learning environment. We begin to develop habit patterns and relational skills that will be essential in relationships with the other sex and, eventually, within marriage.

Same-sex friendships provide a healthy, well-roundedness to our lives, both now and in the future. No one person can meet all our emotional needs, not even a marriage partner. Couples who do not allow friendships outside the marriage or dating relationship end up hurting themselves. In time, through their exclusiveness, they will destroy each other. In *The Friendless American Male*, David Smith says:

> Counselors will quickly tell you that a marriage partner cannot meet all one's needs. A marriage is more healthy when both spouses lead integrated lives. In cases where you find a man who says, "My wife is the only true friend I can turn to," you will also find a wife who says, "I only wish he'd find a friend." A wife cannot meet all the emotional needs of her husband, nor can he meet all of hers.[3]

Throughout my relationship with my wife, Paula, both when we were dating and since we've been married, I've encouraged her to develop her friendships with women. I know that I cannot be everything Paula needs. I'm a man and I can't take the place of a woman nor respond in the way another woman would communicate and respond to Paula. Paula needs her close friendships with other women.

Become a Student of the Other Sex

We need practice in developing strong friendships with the other sex. Men and women are different in many areas — we think and relate differently. So wherever I go, I advocate that people become students of the other sex. Perhaps your response is, "Great! Where is a subject for me to study?" It sounds exciting, and it is, but for a reason other than what you might think. To be such a student is to learn about the intricacies of members of the other sex, to develop heterosexual intimacy built on *awareness*, not necessarily on romance. A good way to do this is to become friends with someone you are not interested in romantically, perhaps someone much older or younger than yourself, or a relative, or a long-term acquaintance. Ask questions about areas that puzzle you. Seek that person's advice. Read books about the other sex to help you understand their concerns, needs, attitudes and thought processes.

What It Takes To Be a Friend

Since the ingredients that go into building deep relationships are learned behaviors, some of those important ingredients to learn are:

1. Communication

Communication is the life blood of a relationship. As long as we communicate openly and honestly, our relationship will grow and mature. When we begin to protect ourselves by sharing only partially, the relationship begins to deteriorate and die. A relationship is only as good as the communication taking place within it.

Different aspects of communication are needed in the process of growth between two people.

First, learn to *share who you are*, that is, what you think, feel, value, love, esteem, hate, fear, desire, hope for, believe in and are committed to. When a person opens up and begins to share these things, that is when the person begins to discover who he or she really is.

One of the benefits of being honest and vulnerable with another person is that we have an opportunity to be accepted unconditionally for who we are. As a result, we experience something of what God's unconditional love for us is like through the relationship.

Second, learn to *work through differences and conflicts*. When conflict arises in a relationship (and it most certainly will at some time), we have the option of striking out, walking out or talking it out. Talking it out establishes longevity in a relationship.

In dealing with conflict, we must make a real effort to understand the other person. What are his or her feelings and thoughts and why does he or she think that way?

Work through differences. Friends who are roommates can have all kinds of differences that need to be worked through. Sometimes it's hard to be patient. "Why didn't they come home on time when they asked me to make the meal?" "Who is going to clean up this mess?"

The temperature of the home or office can be a strong point of disagreement. One may like it cold and the other hot. I had a roommate who loved his room ice cold. In the winter, Frank opened the windows all the way and slept with little clothing under light covers. I liked my room warm. I would go into the hall, turn up the thermostat and go back to bed. Later, Frank would sneak into the hall and turn the thermostat down. In the middle of the night, I would wake up freezing and turn the thermostat higher. One time he faked me out by going down to the basement and turning off the furnace completely. I froze, but never caught on. Now we laugh about it, but at the time it raised our emotional temperatures.

Besides seeking to understand the other person and his or her viewpoint, we need to be willing to listen. Too often we are so busy thinking about what we will say next that we fail to really hear what that person is saying. Listening is an act of recognition. It's an important part of communication that shows you care about the other person and what they have to say. When we listen, we respond to what the person is or isn't saying and to where he or she is coming from. Listening is being involved with the other person mentally and emotionally. It shows that we are not being preoccupied with ourselves.

2. Sacrifice and Commitment

Sacrifice and commitment are qualities you don't hear much about nowadays. Learn to sacrifice — your schedule, your time, your activities, perhaps even your belongings — for the sake of a relationship. There must be give and take in any human relationship and particularly in one involving commitment. For the sake of a friendship, you may decide to do things that you would not choose to do otherwise.

Too often we want the benefits of an intimate friendship without being willing to pay the price of faithfulness and commitment. But we cannot have the benefits without paying the price. Intimacy and commitment go hand in hand.

In any intimate relationship, there may be times when one person will have to do most of the giving. This is the test of loyalty when we are able to look beyond our own needs and stick by our friends. A true friendship will be characterized by mutual loyalty and interdependence.

To see a relationship grow, we need to make the decision to sacrifice and commit ourselves to the other person through good and bad times before the bad times come. The Book of Proverbs says, "A friend loves at all times, and a brother is born for adversity" (Proverbs 17:17).

3. Trust and Trustworthiness

Before we can be committed in a relationship, a trust needs to develop. Faithfulness, a decision we make with our will, is in reality the fruit of trust.

We need to develop the quality of being trustworthy so a person can feel safe with us and know that we will not betray or desert him. Trustworthiness also involves keeping confidences. This allows someone to share inner thoughts or feelings, knowing that these will stop with us and not be broadcast any further. When there is no trust between two people, there is no ability to give of self freely and unreservedly. As a result, the relationship will be undermined.

George Eliot said, "Friendship is the inexpressible comfort of feeling safe with a person having neither to weigh thoughts nor measure words. We can only do this with someone we trust."

4. Acceptance and Respect

If we are unable to accept and respect a friend for who he or she is, with his or her strengths and weaknesses, then we will be trying constantly to change that person.

Everyone has idiosyncrasies and weaknesses. If we can't accept these, then we will put tremendous pressure on both the person and the relationship. Very few relationships can withstand this type of destructive pressure.

Jesus warned us about picking each other apart. "Why do you look at the speck in your brother's eye, but do not notice the log that is in your own eye? . . . First take the log out of your own eye, and then you will see clearly enough to take the speck out of your brother's eye" (Matthew 7:3,5).

Respect is developed when we can put a person's faults and virtues into perspective. Then we can encourage the development of strengths and be patient with that person's weaknesses.

5. Encouragement

Encouraging a friend involves being there and asking God for wisdom to listen, to empathize and to know how to respond. It involves helping your friend see his circumstances from God's perspective.

Encouragement involves not only what we say but what we do for someone. Running errands or taking care of other tasks for the person may relieve some of the weight pressing in on him or her. Encouragement involves time.

It means giving an honest compliment, saying the positive things about another that we often think but neglect to verbalize. Proverbs says "Oil and perfume make the heart glad, so a man's counsel is sweet to his friend" (Proverbs 27:9).

6. Hard Work and Maintenance

Friendship is like riding a bicycle. You either go forward or you fall down. Intimate relationships don't just happen. They falter

unless they are nurtured and maintained. If we want a relationship
to be worth anything, then it takes work from both people involved.

These six aspects are qualities of friendship that Paula and I
focused on and developed in our dating relationship. As a result,
it is now my joy and privilege to be married to my best friend.

In romance and emotional passion, togetherness is so much
better when it is built on friendship, caring, companionship and
learning to get rid of selfishness and self-centeredness.

Bill, a single businessman, told me about his ups and downs
in the business world. At the end of our conversation, he said
that one of the sadnesses of his life was that there was no one to
share his victories and defeats. He was all alone. Because of all
his business problems and debts he said, "I guess there is no one
that would want to marry me. I'll be alone the rest of my life."

Personally, I believe Bill's statement is a mistaken assumption.
Maybe he won't marry for a long time. But he could build good
friendships with people he could care about and just talk to. There
are so many open-hearted people, people who, when you get to
know them, would sacrifice for you. Don't paint yourself into a
corner and say that no one is going to like you and therefore
you're alone. Instead, reach out to build up other people and then
they will build you up.

In my forty-two years of singlehood, I had many problems.
But when I reached out to others, it seemed that my problems
were minimized. When I gave my life away, I found that I had
so much more to give and I received so much more in return.
This is the beginning of relationships.

My advice to Bill was, "When you are interested in dating,
don't just look for a date, look for a friend."

Another guy, Robert, told me, "I judge women before I even
get to know them. I just look at them and decide whether I'm
going to like them or not." How pathetic! Unfortunately, this is
a common tendency — our eyes see what we think we want but
our eyes are often wrong. The person you label as a dud or a
reject could end up providing you with a good relationship.

Paula and I found this out. We knew each other for almost
two years before we married. But I wouldn't recommend our first
date as the way to start a relationship. That first date was a disaster.

Finding My Life-Long Best Friend

I met Paula on a beautiful June afternoon in Fort Collins, Colorado, while I was teaching at Campus Crusade's Institute of Biblical Studies. I was at the medical clinic getting an allergy shot when I saw two women come down the hall in tennis outfits. I don't play tennis. Racquetball is my game. But when one of them sat down next to me, I decided I was interested in tennis. I soon found myself discussing the fine points of the game. During our conversation, I discovered that she was attending the conference, too. But our casual conversation never led to introductions so I didn't get her name.

Three weeks later I saw her in the conference dining room. Nonchalantly, I just "happened" to bump into her. I learned her name and later asked her for a date. But when the date came around, something else upset me so I hardly paid attention to Paula. In fact, for nine months I didn't give her another thought.

Then in April I went to Florida State University for a three-night speaking series called, "Dynamic Relationships." Paula, who worked there for Campus Crusade, was assigned to be my liaison, to drive me to my speaking engagements.

After the speaking series, Paula drove me to the airport. When we stopped for lunch, she asked me if I remembered our date the previous summer. "What date?" I replied. I couldn't remember it! She reminded me of some of the things we did, including the concert we attended. I remembered those things, but to this day I don't remember that she was the one I was with. Obviously, this shocked her, but she was also amused by it. She later told me that, at that point, she decided I must be a real character.

At the concert, I had seen a girl whom I had asked to the concert before I asked Paula. The girl had said she couldn't go. I really liked her. When I saw her there with someone else, my mind went haywire. The rest of the night I didn't say much at all to Paula. All I could think of was how the other girl had "done me wrong."

After that date, the other girls in the dorm asked Paula, "What is Dick like?"

Because I had been so quiet and my mind preoccupied, she answered, "He's a dud."

Isn't that a great way to start a relationship? She thought I was a dud and I couldn't remember her.

Sitting in that restaurant in Tallahassee, Florida, nine months later, sharing these first impressions broke the ice for us. I couldn't believe how dumb I had been.

In the course of the conversation, I asked her what she did in her spare time. She told me she was reading the book, *The Rise and Fall of the Third Reich*. That's a massive book, a real pants presser! That impressed me.

After I left, obviously I had to write to Paula. It was my duty, you understand. In the letter I asked her what she was doing with her time. She replied that, while the students were busy with final exams, she decided to find out something about baseball. When she went to a double-header, she ended up sitting next to the girl friend of a player. The girl explained the fine points of the game to Paula.

It impressed me that Paula wanted to learn about different things. A book about the Second World War and a double-header brought us together. I didn't know what she was like, but I was interested in the mystery of Paula and I wanted to explore her mind. By this time, she was attracted to me, also.

The next summer, at the same Colorado conference, I decided to get to know her better along with some other girls. Actually, my roommate and I decided to date ten different girls that summer, so I had my "Ten Most Wanted" list. At this time, I wasn't looking to marry or settle down. I just wanted to have fun. And fun I had.

After two weeks, I narrowed the field down to two girls, Natalie and Paula. But, while dating Natalie on Friday night, I realized I was miserable. Afterward, I thought, *Why should I waste my time? I thoroughly enjoy being with Paula. She's a lot of fun and I'm interested in knowing more about her.* I decided to pursue our friendship. I wasn't looking for marriage. I simply wanted to gain a special friend. It was exciting for me to be with Paula. It wasn't pressure at all.

After a few weeks, Paula told me, "Dick, we are spending a lot of time together and I don't want you to get the wrong impression. I enjoy you, but I know our relationship could never go anywhere, so I think we should stop dating."

"Well, Paula," I said, "that's all right. I just want to be your friend. If you don't want to date, that's okay. But I have really enjoyed being with you and getting to know you better."

"Really?" she said. "Do you think we can date and still be just friends?"

"Sure, I'm not interested in getting serious or getting married, but I am interested in building a friendship."

We continued to learn about each other, talking about every subject imaginable. One day Paula told her roommate some of the things we had talked about. Her roommate said, "I've been dating my boyfriend for almost two years and we don't discuss the things you do." Paula and I had been open and honest and had enjoyed getting to know the intricacies of the other person.

By the time we married a year later, we were best friends. Our joy in learning about each other and wanting to have an emotional connection just grew and multiplied. Instead of looking for romance, we had looked for friendship. Instead of looking for excitement sexually, we had looked for enjoyment with a companion.

Becoming a student of the other sex allowed us to develop friendships and caring relationships. Many single adults are too quick to cut off potential relationships if the person isn't a prospective mate. Don't be too impatient to get something serious going. Plug away and commit yourselves just to enjoying each other and to becoming friends.

---

1. Which of the purposes of dating are most important to you?

2. What obstacles do you find when trying to become a close friend to someone of the other sex?

3. How do you deal with conflict or differences in your relationships? Do you strike out, walk out or talk it out?

Section One

How to Short-Circuit a Relationship

Chapter Three
Protect Your Heart

From the time we are born, we want and need love. During World War II, in an overcrowded orphanage, physically healthy babies began to die for no apparent reason. Close attention was paid to providing for all their physical needs, but still they died. Finally, it was realized that the children who lived were those who were able to get some loving and cuddling by the overworked orphanage staff. No wonder those who go through life without experiencing intimacy and closeness with others have a difficult time.

Despite the fact that we all desire and need love, many people have a tendency to run from love. Marshall Hodge, in his book, *Your Fear of Love*,[1] states, "We long for expression of love, but frequently, at the critical moment, we pull back. We are afraid of closeness, afraid of love, afraid of the very thing we so desperately desire. Why? Because we don't want to get hurt."

The closer you come to someone emotionally, the greater potential there is for that person to reject or misunderstand you. We don't mind too much if a stranger shows a lack of interest in us, but if the ones we love most do not respond to us positively, we are devastated.

Another writer, Hugo Black, in his book, *Friendship*,[2] says, "Every relationship means risk, but we must take the risk; for while nearly all our sorrows come from our connection with others, nearly all our joys have the same source." We want to overcome loneliness, to have intimacy, to experience deep friendship, but we don't want any pain to come with it.

Despite the fact that my wife Paula and I love each other deeply, we have found that we still manage to say or do things that hurt each other, even though we don't mean to. We've had to apologize to each other many times since we've been married. That's part of the reality of life. There is no such thing as painless love.

A friend of mine told me how, as early as junior high school, he had learned to protect his heart. He would give candy to a girl to show her that he liked her, rather than saying the words, "I like you." She might reject his words of affection, but she wasn't likely to reject the candy.

The desire to protect ourselves doesn't stop after adolescence. Following one of my talks on relationships, a woman in her twenties told me, "I'm taking steps never to be hurt again."

"Then, Joyce, you're taking steps never to love again," I warned her. "No matter what you do, you can't have love without experiencing some pain."

"Why not?" she said. "I want love, but I don't want to be hurt by another guy again."

In one way or another all of us have suffered from past relationships. Through these experiences our hearts carry the emotional scars and bruises that result. Because of these, we often develop defenses to protect ourselves from future hurt and pain. These defensive roles, games and masks become a natural reflex action for us. Not only do they destroy our ability to develop intimacy in our relationships with others, but they also destroy our ability to grow personally.

Trying to Control Love

We want intimacy and yet we are afraid, so we give people a *double signal*. On one hand, we signal to them, "Come closer," while on the other hand we signal, "Stay away." We subtly communicate, "You're an attractive person and I want to be needed and liked by you. I want closeness." At the same time, we shy away by hinting, "I don't want you to get involved in things that might bring out some of my vulnerable spots."

We want both to develop and to avoid a close relationship. It's like stepping on the gas pedal of your car with one foot while holding your other on the brake. The car shakes a little and then it stalls. In much the same way, a lot of relationships stall and die.

The Wall of Protection

To protect our hearts, we *build walls* around them. We want to keep people from getting in to hurt us. But remember, the same wall that keeps people out also keeps us trapped inside by ourselves. When we build walls, we force ourselves to handle our problems and struggles alone — and that is loneliness. Being alone is not loneliness. A sense of facing life by yourself is loneliness.

We build these walls of protection over the years by avoiding emotional closeness with people, by steering conversation away from subjects or feelings that are potentially painful to us and even by being offended when such subjects are approached.

Have you sometimes felt like two people? One is the exterior you, the person everyone sees and talks to. The other is the deep down inside you that few people ever see. Others rarely see this second you because the learning-to-open-up process is hard to go through. Often, we don't like our deep-down-inside person, so we keep him or her hidden, for fear others will reject that person. So, instead of risking, we build walls around our hearts.

Robert Frost aptly said, "Do not build a wall until you know what you are walling in and what you are walling out."

Denying Our Need for Love

Some people try to protect their hearts by denying that they really want or need someone else. Our society's emphasis on independence makes it appear that to admit we need each other is a sign of weakness.

After years of looking fruitlessly for the "one woman" for me, I finally began to pray that God would take away my desire for a wife. I didn't know how to handle the deep loneliness or emotions I felt down inside. After awhile, I realized that my prayer was asking God to make me abnormal.

I'm grateful God didn't answer those prayers. Instead, He gave me the strength to handle the pressure and the loneliness. As I faced and accepted my need, He brought other friends and interests into my life to ease my loneliness and to provide for my need to be loved. Then, eventually, He did bring the woman perfectly suited for me into my life.

The Testing Game

By testing others' feelings toward us, we try to protect our hearts. We are always watching their responses to us — the way they look at us, how much they talk to us or how they react to what we say or do. Based on that, we make a decision about how much of ourselves we will reveal to them and how much we will give of ourselves in the relationship.

A woman may think, "If he calls me several times this week, then I'll know he cares." A man may decide, "If she smiles and acts friendly when I talk with her, then I'll know she's interested and I'll ask her out." There's always a holding back until the other person passes your test. If both people play this game, the relationship may never get started.

Communicating feelings, without knowing if the other person will reciprocate, represents a real leap of faith. Some may resist any possibility of hurt or rejection because of hurt in the past.

The Turtle Syndrome

To protect their hearts, people become overly cautious and get caught up in what I call the *turtle syndrome*. The neck goes out, the head looks around, and, if anything potentially dangerous is seen, the neck goes right back in again.

When we have been rejected and disappointed, there is a tendency to project that bad experience on all others of that sex. We are convinced, "*They're* all the same."

Quite often, a man won't ask a woman out because he might get turned down, rejected. He would rather sit at home all weekend than take that chance. If a woman would give him some subtle, but definite encouragement to do so, he might be more inclined to take the chance. But, of course, the woman doesn't want to be too blatant in showing her interest, in case the man doesn't want to ask her out. She shows only the same polite interest that she might show any person, just in case he isn't interested. Neither of them want to "make fools of themselves."

As a single person, I stayed at home many weekends because I didn't want to face the possibility of being turned down for a date. I thought, *if I don't ask, I can't be hurt.* But my timidity resulted in many lonely hours.

To avoid exposing the deep-down-inside person, some people retreat into a shell of busyness. They marry their work and become workaholics. They become totally involved in their jobs, so that the distraction of being busy keeps them from facing themselves or others on a deep level.

As a protection against getting too close to other people, a friend of mine got so involved in his work that, eventually, he had a nervous breakdown. As head of a large organization, he had little time for anyone or anything else. After awhile, he began to have all kinds of pain and physical symptoms that led to the breakdown. It is impossible to hide from others or from ourselves without negative consequences.

Finally, if we do arrange a date, we still act like emotional turtles by sticking only to small talk. We bottle up our feelings, fears, dreams and sorrows and end up with superficial relationships. As a result, we relate only to how the person looks, acts and reacts. We remain attracted only to the person's outward appearance, including his or her sensuality, because that's all we know of that person.

No wonder a typical date is getting something to eat, going to a movie and then making out. There's no risk, no sharing, no giving, no true companionship. The person experienced in this type of casual dating has a hard time interacting with someone on a deeper level. The habit of hiding in a shell takes a lot of effort to break.

Giving in the Wrong Way

In *The New Celibacy*, Gabrielle Brown says, "Sex is, in fact, often used as an excuse for actually avoiding intimacy. If one is afraid of the surrender required for growing intimacy, sex can be used as a cover for that fear."[3] Some people protect their hearts by letting sex communicate for them. They *give their bodies* to people but never give their inner selves — their minds and hearts.

People also protect their hearts by *giving things* instead of themselves. They readily give material gifts, but never give of themselves emotionally. It's too frightening to be so vulnerable.

Many parents do this with their children. A number of my friends have told me that their parents never sat down with them to find out what they were like deep inside. Nor would their parents readily share about themselves. These friends had to judge their parents' love by the material things they were given, a poor substitute for true intimate love.

The Great Cover-Up

Other people *hide behind their strengths* or positive personality traits to avoid exposing their weaknesses and vulnerabilities. "So what's wrong with that? After all, shouldn't you put your best foot forward?" But if only your best foot is put forward, your weak foot never has a chance to become stronger. Other people see you as only half a person. For example:

Helen enjoys asking questions and finding out about other people. Asking puts her in control of conversations. Although they like Helen's attention, they never find out anything about Helen. She is always playing the part of the counselor without revealing what is going on inside her own life and heart.

Tom is a comedian, the life of the party. He uses his strength — jokes and laugther — to keep people at arm's length. In this way, he avoids letting others know what's really going on inside of him. Many famous comedians are people who are or have been desperately lonely and fearful of others.

Lynn hides behind knowledge. She has a ready answer for everything including Bible verses for any situation. She wants to be helpful so categorizing solutions for all situations is a priority to her. However, Lynn doesn't allow a hurting person to feel any pain or grief. She is too quick to throw them pat answers even from Scripture, instead of being sensitive to what they are feeling.

God's word is powerful and we need it to overcome our problems. But when hurting people try to change immediately from a reaction of sorrow to one of joy, they may find themselves with deeper emotional troubles later on. Like Lynn, we need to learn that what a hurting person needs first is someone who can comfort and empathize so that the hurt and sorrow can come out, not be denied. As Romans 12:15 says, "Weep with those who weep."

Lynn has a hard time allowing other people to feel emotions and pain because she can't face her own hurts and sorrows. She denies the reality that people need to feel suffering because she doesn't want to face her own struggles. Lynn fears that, if she faces her own problems and can't overcome them, it would prove a devastating blow to what she relies on as her strength — her knowledge, which she assumes is wisdom. It has been said that knowledge plus experience equals wisdom. Lynn refuses to "experience" or face the ups and down of life. If she did, she would have more wisdom in dealing with people. Others may admire her positive answers for every situation, but they know her as only half a person, one who faces life with the mind but not with the emotions.

Barriers to Intimacy

Let's look at the fears that cause us to protect our hearts.

1. The Fear of Rejection.

As John Powell says, "I am afraid to tell you who I am, because, if I tell you who I am, you may not like who I am and that's all I have."[4] What a scary and vulnerable position that can be. If we share who we are, then we have nowhere to hide.

If people we loved hurt us in the past, we fear that history will repeat itself and that we might find ourselves devastated again. The old song, written by Burt Bacharach, echoes our sentiment: "I'll Never Fall in Love Again." It may sound wise to say, *Never Again*, but we make a crippling mistake when we cut ourselves off from the rich relationships that God wants to bring into our lives, even if those involve some hurt along the way.

2. The Fear of Dependency

Men often fear being sucked into a smothering relationship with a woman, which would limit their freedom. Women fear having their identity submerged in a relationship with a man.

3. The Fear of Facing One's Loveless Life

A Christian psychotherapist in Dallas finds that persons approaching the possibility of real love and intimacy will refuse it because they have never known it before. Subconsciously, they realize, that if they experience love and intimacy now, they face the reality that their lives have been desperately void of such previously. They are likely to think, *As I let you get close to me, I am overwhelmed with the realization that I've never been loved this way before. It feels as if the anguish of my empty heart will shatter it.*

It is difficult to face the fact that one's whole life has been lived bankrupt of real love. Instead of realized emptiness motivating the person to respond to love never given before, the person runs from it. If one keeps a distance, that realization won't have to be faced.

Fear causes us to be self-protecting, while love is self-giving. Fear causes us to be preoccupied with self. Our fears, loneliness and emotional pain become the focus of our attention. We cannot be self-giving because we are turned inward, busy protecting ourselves.

Fears destroy our ability to fully sense the love that others show us. Self-centeredness and self-absorption isolate us from others and deepen our loneliness and pain.

I saw this when I was in college involved in a ministry to people on skid row. I used to talk to Sam about the Bible but the old man knew the Bible better than I did. If I started to quote a verse to him, he would finish quoting it. Yet he refused to open his life to God or to trust God to change his life. He didn't want God to control what he was used to controlling — his miserable, failed life. Sam was afraid to open himself up to God or anyone else because he had been hurt before. He couldn't see that trying to protect his vulnerability and trusting no one, in reality, made him all the more vulnerable to the onslaughts of life. He was his own prisoner.

Too many of us are like Sam. We try to achieve safety and happiness by protecting ourselves. But, eventually, self-absorption leads to a life that is no bigger than ourselves and that, my friend, is true misery.

Breaking Down the Wall

What can we do to break down the wall of protection we have built around our hearts? There are a number of steps that help bring down that wall.

1. Accept God's acceptance of you.

His love for you is infinitely strong. Realize that your security is found in Him and in His eternal family — the body of believers, the church. You can be confident that He is not going to leave you or forsake you (Hebrews 13:5). He understands you. He didn't make a mistake when he created you (Jeremiah 1:5). When you came along, He didn't sneeze. He wasn't on a vacation. He didn't say, "Oops, I didn't do a good job on that one!" There may be things about yourself that you don't like, but God has not, in any way, looked down and tried to work you over before accepting you (Romans 5:8).

2. Look at Christ's example of vulnerability.

When Jesus was on this earth, He opened Himself to criticism and broken promises. Even though He was God, He was willing to open Himself to people. Many loved Him and many hurt Him but He didn't try to protect His heart. How could He open Himself like that? Just because He was God? No. Jesus was not fearful of being hurt by those He loved because He knew how completely His Father loved Him and He was secure in that. No matter who rejected him, the Father would always accept and love Him.

That same fulfilling love that Jesus knew is ours. In John 17:23 and 26 (NIV), Jesus prayed to His Father that the world might know that the Father "loved them [us, his disciples] even as you have loved me" and that "the love you have for me may be in them." As we come to realize that love, the fear of rejection and even rejection itself, will not devastate us.

3. Deal with the fears and hurts.

Be brutally honest with yourself. Do you have difficulties relating intimately? What are you afraid of? Ask the Lord to help you overcome these fears. It may take a long time for some emotional scars to heal, but the Lord wants you to move ahead with His courage in spite of those wounds. In that way the fears will decrease. Dealing with your pains and hurts from the past is important in helping to release you from your present fears.

4. Share your life with others.

Begin to open up and share who you are including your failures and growth. The more secure you become in God's love and acceptance, the more you can risk rejection. Reveal yourself to others first, then they will feel comfortable enough to reveal themselves to you. As they see you accept yourself as an imperfect person on the road to maturity, they will realize that you are free to accept their imperfections as well.

Years ago, I started a small fellowship group with nine other men. We called it our CELL group — Christians Encouraging, Learning and Loving. We met on Tuesday nights and Friday mornings and we went on camping trips and played basketball together. With them, I could let down my hair and reveal who I really was and where I was in my life and Christian growth. We learned not only about each other but about ourselves. We became intimate friends for life.

5. Reach out and help others.

As the men in my CELL group became involved in each others' lives, we began to reach out to help people outside our group as well. This experience formed the basis for my book, *The 31-Day Experiment*. The book is a 31-day biblical study guide with ways to apply the passages by reaching out to others. It is designed to help Christians become consistent in their daily walk with God. *The 31-Day Experiment* helps develop the habit of looking for ways to help others.[5]

6. Let others help you.

I find a lot of people who are willing to give help but are not willing to receive it. They are always the first to lend a helping hand in time of need, but they themselves refuse to be helped. I know a mother who is always giving her time and money to her children, but she has a hard time accepting anything they offer. That is a subtle form of pride. Often, such people feel overly responsible not only for self but for others. Allow others to know your needs and to give to you.

Some people are walking hypochondriacs, demanding that people help them constantly. They take but rarely give help. Such people usually are blind to how much they sap others. But most of us err on the other side, not allowing others to give to us.

As we begin to work through the barriers that motivate us to self protection, those walls around our hearts will start to collapse. Then we begin to become whole people, able to love deeply and be loved deeply.

---

1. Why do you think people have a tendency to run from love?

2. What do you need to do to break down the walls surrounding your heart?

3. How does accepting God's acceptance of us affect our relationships with others?

Chapter Four
Press for Instant Intimacy

When I lived in a small midwestern city, I became so irritated at traffic lights that I checked the amount of time different lights stayed red. I avoided the longer ones. To my surprise, I discovered that the average light stayed red all of forty-five seconds! You would have thought it was close to forty-five minutes, considering how often I became impatient waiting for a green light. Many people have had similar feelings. *Wait* is a word we modern people don't like to hear, let alone experience.

We're members of the instant gratification generation, an age that expects immediate access to every desire. We push a button and a computer immediately gives us information that once took hours to research in libraries or stacks of records.

We have fast foods, instant breakfasts, microwave ovens, anything to cut the time and work necessary to meet our needs and wants. If we have to wait five minutes for a hamburger at a restaurant, we consider the service slow.

We have disposable everything — from diapers to eating utensils, from drink cans to razors — just so we don't have to take time to care for the items that make our lives more convenient. We use and toss, use and toss. We get irritated if anything slows us down. We don't like to wait. We are impatient people.

In the same way, many of us want the building of relationships to be quick, exciting and without hindrances. We want to feel good now and we don't want to think about the consequences. We want closeness, fun and thrills, but no commitment. We go to the bars, health clubs and even to church singles groups, to pick up someone or be picked up. When it's over, we know that all we've done is used or touched someone's body, but we've never touched their souls.

We, the instant gratification generation, choose the immediate satisfaction of needs, rather than waiting for better solutions in the future. It's very difficult for us to put off momentary pleasure for lasting satisfaction. Intimacy takes time. It takes vulnerability. It takes commitment. It takes trust. But these are not qualities valued or easily developed in society today.

Though sex involves all of who you are, it doesn't require love. Unfortunately sex and love are often used interchangeably. When we confuse these two, we may satisfy our passions but we end up with an empty heart. We want love and closeness, but often we indulge in only a frustratingly "physical" experience. The result can be disillusionment. Sex is not the answer to the search for enjoyable and lasting intimacy.

Life's Five-Pointed Star

Each of us has five significant parts to our lives — the physical, emotional, mental, social and spiritual. All of these are designed to work together harmoniously, giving us happiness and fulfillment. When they don't work in harmony, we experience frustration, emptiness, and, sometimes, a burned-out feeling.

When the need for intimacy in a relationship isn't met, we look for an instant solution. Where do we find it? In the physical, mental, social, emotional or spiritual part of our relationship? Usually, it's the physical. It's easier to be physically intimate with someone than to be intimate in any of the other four areas. You can become physically intimate in an hour or half hour. It just depends upon the urge! But eventually you discover that this provides only momentary relief for a much deeper need. In fact, physical intimacy by itself is not intimacy at all. It's only a detour around true intimacy.

Gina was dating Bryan. The more they got to know each other, especially in the back of Bryan's van, the more they realized they wanted each other physically. One night they culminated their sexual desires in intercourse, which produced tremendous frustration in Gina's heart. She had exposed her body but had not received what she wanted — true closeness to the one she thought she loved. Their relationship eventually ended in disappointment and guilt.

The more a couple gets involved physically, the less they talk and the more shallow interaction they have in other areas of their lives. Too often, physical involvement merely means that two self-centered people are seeking satisfaction for self-centered desires. Genuine love and intimacy are missing. Sex is used as a shortcut to love but the detour ends up as a dead-end road. You defeat the reason you want intimacy, which is to find lifelong satisfaction.

The Law of Diminishing Returns

At the bottom of all this is "the law of diminishing returns." Concerning dating couples and their sexual involvement, this law proclaims that the more you do it, the less satisfying it is.

The following graph illustrates this. The vertical line represents the level of excitement in a relationship, the horizontal line the amount of time the relationship has been in effect. When a relationship is new, the graph line goes up sharply when the man first puts his arm around the woman or they exchange kisses. At the beginning, it's an exciting new adventure with one another. In essence, they are saying, I like you.

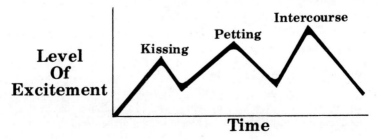

After awhile, the hugs and kisses become a habit and the level of excitement drops again. The graph line flattens out and then begins to go down. Then activities evolve into light petting, which is exhilarating. Again, the thrill increases and the curve shoots up.

When this no longer satisfies, they move into heavy petting. For the moment, they feel satisfied in the rush of passion and the warm closeness that follows. Eventually, that too is unable to satisfy and becomes frustrating. Each person begins to feel unfulfilled. Each realizes that there is still no sense of complete oneness.

Eventually, the couple is likely to culminate their desires in sexual intercourse and then there is passion and release. But unexpectedly, even at this stage, dissatisfaction, disappointment and disillusionment result and the graph line goes down, down, down, into the negative zone.

From all we hear today, sexual intercourse should be the apex, the greatest experience of life. Psychologist Dr. Henry Brandt, however, describes a familiar pattern:

> Frequently I listen to young men and women who have had experiences with heavy petting or premarital sex relations. They describe a similar pattern, saying, "First, there was great pleasure in it. Then I started hating myself. Next, I found myself hating my partner and we ended up embarrassed and ashamed, and then we broke up and became enemies."[1]

What a way to end a promising relationship. It starts with excitement and hope, but it ends with bitterness. In fact, sexual burnout is the primary reason why dating relationships are destroyed. As a result, Dr. Joyce Brothers has said that sex is now about as satisfying as a sneeze.[2]

The Morning-After Syndrome

This pattern is what I call the "morning after syndrome." A sexually active couple awake to find that intimacy is fleeting. The sexual relationship doesn't satisfy them any more and what they end up with is not what they really wanted. Realizing that genuine love and intimacy cannot be obtained instantly, they find themselves still searching for harmony in the five areas of life that affect intimacy.

No matter what our friends and the media tell us, the driving desire of each human being is not for sex or romance; it is for true intimacy.

Gabrielle Brown puts it this way:

> Most of us decide in favor of being sexual as much as possible because we've been taught that sex is the road to personal fulfillment. This is one of the most destructive myths about sex — that there is such a thing as permanent fulfillment on the sexual level. No matter how great an orgasm one has or how great an orgasm one's partner has, sex does not bring fulfillment. And if something more permanent is desired in the expression of love and one does not ever experience it, one may feel unfulfilled, even saddened, by the sexual act.[3]

This may happen because, as Elisabeth Haich observed:

> Sexuality mimics love. It compels tenderness and embraces, it forces the lovers to hug one another, to allay one another's pain through the revelations of sexuality, as when true love is exchanged. What follows such experiences? Disappointments, a bitter after-taste, mutual accusations or bleak loneliness, feelings of exploitation and defilement. Neither of the two gave true love but only expected to receive it, therefore, neither received it![4]

Sexuality activity can be very deceptive because it gives a feeling of intimacy, but it is false. You are tricked into thinking more intimacy exists than really does. We fall in love with love and passion rather than with the person as he really is. What is going on is the feeding of each other's needs and self-involvement, but not true satisfying intimacy.

God's Sexual Psychology

Since God created us with our emotional and sexual make-up, He is *the* expert on the subject of sex. He's the one who thought up the whole idea in the first place. When God speaks on the subject of sex, He gives us principles to live by. These are not designed to spoil our fun but to give us the best kind of intimacy. God *always* wants to *protect* us from harm and to *provide* us with the most satisfying sex life.

It did not take modern psychology to discover the problems involved with sex outside of true love and total commitment in marriage. The Bible warned us of that thousands of years ago. When God created it, He knew that the physical feelings involved in the sexual act would drive us toward it. He wanted it that way, among other reasons, in order to continue the human race.

Sex and Procreation

God gave us commandments to keep sex within marriage so that the love of two people could produce another life that could grow up in the secure, loving and intimate environment of a family. Such an environment is crucial for the development of healthy personalities. Procreation within a family environment is a major reason not only for the sex drive, but for keeping it within marriage. However, it is not the only reason for God's commandments against adultery and fornication.

In the past, continuing the human race was the main reason "responsible" people waited until marriage to consummate the sexual act. Once contraceptives and legal abortions became available, that reason for abstaining from sex without marriage became a much weaker one. Pregnancy was still a risk, but a much lesser one. Abortion was still a physical and social risk, but far less so. No longer did the high degree of physical risk keep two people who were attracted to one another from considering sex as just an enjoyable pastime. All along there had been other reasons for keeping sexual relations within marriage, but these could be ignored as long as the physical risk and resulting social risk acted as deterrents.

Sex and Unity

God created our physical bodies, our ability to have sexual relations and the physical feelings it produces, but He also created the emotions that result from sex and our desire for openness and commitment to one person.

Another reason, then, for keeping sex within marriage was that God designed it to produce unity between a man and woman totally committed to each other. Genesis 2:24,25 says: "For this cause a man shall leave his father and his mother, and shall cleave to his wife; and they shall become one flesh. And the man and his wife were both naked and were not ashamed."

"They shall become one flesh" is not only physical oneness but also an emotional, intellectual and spiritual bonding that sex provides. Sexual intercourse is a whole-person act. Only a small part of it is the physical aspect. Sex was never intended by God to be merely a "physical" experience. He created sex to have emotional effects, even on a subconscious level. He created it to involve the total person, so that it would be both the culmination and expression of the deep intimacy that has been and will continue to be developed between a couple throughout their lives together.

The Old Testament word for intercourse is *knowledge*. To have sex, in biblical terms, is *to know* your partner. The implication is that sex involves not only a physical nakedness but a total nakedness — knowing the person on all levels, openly and vulnerably.

Within marriage, there is the freedom to give ourselves completely, unreservedly, feeling "naked and unashamed" before our mate. Because of the lifetime commitment, a complete love-trust relationship can be developed without the fear of being judged as acceptable or unacceptable by our mate. Lifetime acceptability has been adhered to within the marriage commitment, so there is no fear of desertion and rejection.

To have sex is to give yourself away. God wants to protect us from giving ourselves away to someone who will not be there for a lifetime with us. Once you have given yourself away, you can never take yourself back. When the person to whom you have given yourself walks out of your life, something of you goes too.

When I was at the University of Indiana, I was required to attend a human sexuality conference at which a woman psychologist spoke. The group included planned parenthood people, doctors, nurses, professors and graduate students like myself. During one afternoon session, the psychologist spoke of virginity. She started telling a lot of jokes and everyone got a big laugh. She was putting virginity down and making fun of it. I didn't laugh. I'd bet a billion dollars God didn't laugh either. Do you know why? Virginity is the only thing in our lives that we can give to one person one time only. It's the most precious physical and emotional gift we can give to anyone.

In sex we expose ourselves in the most vulnerable way possible. Our innermost being is unprotected as at no other time. Within marriage this can cause a deepening of the relationship and growth of the two people. Outside the protective shelter of marriage we open ourselves to the deepest heartaches possible. God wants to protect our hearts, our minds and our innermost being.

Sex and Pleasure

A third purpose for which God created sex was to increase the pleasure of marriage. God designed sex to produce and enhance relational intimacy, with pleasure being the by-product.

God knows that real sexual enjoyment and fulfillment come when we experience total freedom in a relationship. The degree to which we are unable to experience emotional and physical freedom will be the degree to which the enjoyment is diminished.

In the marriage relationship there can be *total* sexual freedom because only in a total, lifetime commitment is freedom possible on *all* levels of life — emotional, mental, social, spiritual and physical. There is safety and security. A person can therefore give himself to his mate without fear of abandonment.

There is also total freedom from guilt in sex within marriage. You can know that God smiles on and is pleased with your sexual relationship. God never intended us to be ashamed of our bodies, of sexual touching or of anything related to the sexual relationship between a husband and wife. We can let go of inhibitions and totally enjoy every aspect of sexual union.

Outside of marriage, guilt eats away at the individuals until the relationship is either destroyed or crippled. Outside of marriage, sexual pleasure becomes selfish gratification instead of a beautiful expression of giving to one another.

True sexual enjoyment comes only with emotional freedom stimulated by lifetime commitment and the absence of guilt. Yet along with this, a deep friendship with communication and trans- parency must be present. When we are able to be ourselves totally and to be emotionally "naked" without fear, then we experience the freedom that allows us to give of ourselves to the relationship. The ability to give ourselves freely, completely and unreservedly on all levels is crucial to experiencing the joy and pleasure God intended sex to bring to a husband and wife.

When we have sex outside the boundaries that God has set up for our protection and provision, we end up cheating ourselves. God is more concerned about our happiness, our relationships and our sexual fulfillment than we are. He wants the very best for us, not only today, but also in the future. He doesn't want us to lack any good thing. This is why God has clearly said no to sex outside the protective walls of marriage.

Three Kinds of Love

What is true love? Songs have been sung about it. Poets have written about it. People have expressed it to their partners. But it still remains elusive. By looking at the divorce statistics and unhappy homes, we can see that few marriage relationships achieve it.

In *Givers, Takers, and Other Kinds of Lovers*, Josh McDowell and Paul Lewis express the essence of sex and true love:

> And for all its apparent staying power and lasting attraction, sex is fragile. It takes time and needs security. It only really blossoms when enjoyed in the context of genuine unconditional love. In fact, you'll never discover ultimate sex until you have understood how to give and receive ultimate love."[5]

In Greek, the original language of the New Testament, three different words are translated *love* in English. One is the word *eros*. It is a very self-centered, sexual love. Bluntly stated, *eros* has this attitude: "I like me, you like me; we now both like the same person!" The second word for love is *phileo*. It is a brotherly love, back and forth, between two people — good friends. "I like you, you like me." The third word is *agape*. This is a total, selfless, giving love that does not demand or require a response from the other person, the person loved.

The way we usually love is to start with *eros*. We see someone who turns us on. We want to get to know them in order to have a lot of fun. We may eventually grow into the *phileo* stage of love with them. But we rarely get to the *agape* stage because we are self-centered and insecure, and we want to protect our hearts.

The only person who has ever exhibited pure *agape* love — giving total love before receiving anything in return — is God. In fact, God always starts with *agape* love. He says, "This is [agape] love; not that we [agape] loved God, but that he [agape] loved us and sent his Son as an atoning sacrifice for our sins. Dear friends, since God so [agape] loved us, we also ought to [agape] love one another. No one has ever seen God; but if we [agape] love each other, God lives in us and his [agape] love is made complete in us" (1 John 4:10-12, NIV).

Three-Person Intimacy

To bring God into a relationship seems foreign to all that our culture tells us, yet I believe that real intimacy with another person can be found only when there is, first of all, true agape intimacy with the Creator.

God knows all about each of us. There is not one thing He does not know or understand. God wants us to have intimacy with Him as well as with others. As the Creator of all there is, including sex, He must know the best plan for us to get the greatest fulfillment from it. God is not out to make us miserable. He loves us and wants us to be happy. Our society has taken what God has said about love, sex, and intimacy and has changed it into mere emotions and feelings. Love is more than emotions and it is much more than a good feeling. The love God wants us to have is exciting, fulfilling and lasting. But it can be obtained only through having, first, a close relationship with Him.

But how does this work? How does having intimacy with God affect intimacy with others, particularly with those of the other sex?

To understand God's perspective of love, we must forget what our society tells us about love and intimacy and adopt a new frame of mind. Since the beginning, God has tried to tell people that He loves them. But when the God of the universe, the Creator of us all, says I (*agape*) love you, what does that include? Here are only a few of the many elements of God's love for us.

God's (agape) *love is eternal.* He tells us through the ancient prophet, Jeremiah, "I have loved you with an everlasting love" (Jer. 31:3). God's love is never going to leave us, and that's exciting.

God's (agape) *love is kind.* The word *loving-kindness* is used 180 times throughout the Old Testament to show God's attitude of love and kindness toward people. If God were out to make us miserable, do you think He would continually tell of His lovingkindness — 180 times?

God's (agape) *love is forgiving.* Each of us is self-centered which is what the Bible calls sin. This sin separates us from God and His love. The Bible tells us, "If we confess our sins, He is faithful and righteous to forgive us our sins, and to cleanse us from all unrighteousness" (1 John 1:9). Not only does God forgive our sins, but He forgets them and cleanses us when we respond to Him.

God's (agape) *love is giving.* God loved us so much that He allowed Jesus Christ to die for our sins so that we might be cleansed from them. A very familiar Bible verse says, "For God so loved the world, that He gave His only begotten Son, that whoever believes in Him should not perish, but have eternal life" (John 3:16). To give Jesus Christ over to death, in order to pave the way for us to live eternally with Him, shows how very great God's love is for us.

God's *(agape)* love is totally different from what society defines as love. We can experience *agape* love when we come into a relationship with God. God tells us that His forgiveness and eternal love are ours simply by putting our faith in Him. This love is His gift to us. If we refuse this gift, we cut ourselves off from finding lasting fulfillment, true intimacy and eternal life.

Once we trust Him for His love and forgiveness, we begin to experience a personal relationship and growing intimacy with Him that lasts not only a lifetime but an eternity. This relationship starts when we put our faith in Christ, "Lord Jesus, I know I am a self-centered person and that I need You. You are God and yet You gave Your life for me. I want You to forgive me of my self-centeredness and sin. I put my faith and confidence in You and receive You into my life. I ask You to give me a whole new way of life and, through Your love for me, to make me the kind of person You want me to be."

Whether you have just made this commitment to God or did it a long time ago, you need to understand what type of love God has for you. You may think His love for you is conditional, dependent on whether you always live within His perfect will for you. No matter how you rate your performance record with God, know that His (*agape*) love for you is always total. If you rebel, He will discipline you. But it does not diminish His love.

When you realize this, you will know that you are totally loved. You don't need to reach out desperately to others to receive love. You have unconditional (*agape*) love from God, full and flowing over, enough to give to others, whether or not you receive love from them. You realize that love and intimacy are much more than what you have experienced before. Love and intimacy involve the whole of life and, when including the sexual area, are meant to be experienced through a lifelong marriage commitment of total trust.

---

1. Why is it so easy to not think about the consequences of a sexual relationship?

2. In what way does sex become a detour to love?

3. How has God protected you and provided the best for you?

Chapter Five
Say Yes and Be Sorry

Ernest Hemingway once said, "What is moral is what you feel good after and what is immoral is what you feel bad after."

The question remains, How long after? Sometimes the most devastating consequences of sexual immorality don't show up until some time has passed. Unfortunately, many people find that the long-range consequences of sex outside marriage produce problems that far surpass the temporary ecstasy they felt during the sexual experience.

When God commanded us to limit sexual experience to marriage, He did it because He loves us and wants only the best for us. He knows the attraction of sex. He created it.

Within God's protective boundaries of marriage, sex can be a warm expression of a couple's commitment to one another, bonding further their cohesiveness and oneness. It will culminate, on the physical level, a union that is already developing on all other levels.

A yes to sex outside of marriage winds up being regret. A person may not always trace the pain and consequences to its

source — a misuse of God's gift of sex. God gave us many
warnings against adultery and fornication, not to limit our happiness,
but to maximize it. Those who do not understand or refuse to
believe God's warnings often find that sex can turn into a monster.

Jimmy Williams, President of Probe Ministries, a Christian
"think tank," said in his book, *Why Wait 'Til Marriage?* "I've
never met any individuals who were sorry for saving their sexual
experience until they were able to give themselves to a special
person in marriage. I have, however, met and counseled with
scores of people who regretted that they did not."[1]

The NBC documentary, "Second Thoughts on Being Single,"
included the statement, "The sexual revolution has reduced men
and women's intimacy to the moral equivalent of fast food. Women
are finding that 'junk sex' is no more satisfying than junk food
and that sexual liberation has not yet met expectations."[2]

Not only has sexual liberation not been satisfying and not
met expectations, but it also has left in its path countless broken
and ravaged lives. People are unprepared for the devastating results
of the misuse of sex. They extol the pleasures of ending a date
in bed and advocate premarital sex as the satisfaction to passion,
bringing unparalleled happiness. All the while, they are ignorant,
or refuse to recognize, what the longer-lasting consequences may
be to themselves and to their partners.

In this chapter, we'll take a look at many of the painful,
long-range consequences of sex outside marriage. After reading
about them, some of you, who are sexually-experienced singles,
may wonder if there is any hope for you to have a fulfilling life
and marriage in the future. God always provides a way to heal.
Although the road to healing may have its own trials, there is
hope for peace, happiness and fulfillment when you confess your
wrong actions, thoughts and attitudes to God. Ask Christ to lead
you in the power of the Holy Spirit to a life that is within His
good and intended will for you.

Psychological Consequences

When I lecture on the subject, "Sex and the Search for
Intimacy," I've noticed that facts and statistics on the physical and
social consequences of sex outside marriage usually don't bother

people who are sexually active. They assume that science and medicine will take care of venereal disease and that contraceptives or luck will prevent unwanted pregnancies. And if, heaven forbid, something does go wrong, they'll think about that later.

However, when I mention the negative psychological or relational aspects, they take notice. There are no easy solutions to the following consequences of sex outside marriage.

1. Guilt

When you violate your conscience or break God's moral law, guilt floods your mind and heart. It is an intellectual and emotional response to wrong actions and attitudes. The guilt is both psychological and spiritual.

In his book, *Why Wait 'Till Marriage?*, Jimmy Williams writes that guilt can produce devastating results in human behavior. "It is anger turned inward, producing depression, a lowered self-esteem, and fatigue. Researchers find the highest prevalence of nervous symptoms among those with the least sexual restraint. Further, chastity and virginity contribute very little to sexual problems; unsatisfying relationships, guilt, hostility toward the opposite sex and low self-esteem do. In short, there are no scars where there have been no wounds."[3]

Sometimes, counselors find that wounds have been covered up like a scab over a festering sore. The conscience can be blunted to where there are no guilt feelings. Guilt has been submerged in a sea of rationalization and excuses, called guilt-desensitization. By indulging in something over and over, the conscience has been desensitized until it no longer bothers the person, at least not directly. Instead, the guilt comes out in other ways that seem unrelated to the original guilt-producing behavior. We become so familiar with what we are doing that the boundaries of right and wrong become blurred. Wrong no longer seems wrong but O.K., so right and good.

Wayne told me about his own experience after I spoke to his singles group. From his first sexual experience, he found temporary pleasure. Afterward, he was overwhelmed by guilt and disgust at himself. He knew that intercourse was meant for marriage. He was so upset by his actions that when he got home, he ran to the bathroom and vomited. Guilt flooded his emotions.

The next weekend, however, he and his girl friend had intercourse again. This time, the pleasure was not followed by such extreme guilt reactions. Afterward, he felt miserable but didn't head for the bathroom. Eventually, after repeated sexual encounters, his guilt subsided completely. However, as time went on, a deeper repressed guilt and confusion about his whole life began tearing him apart.

Acknowledged or not, guilt is still a destroyer. Repressed guilt can lead to depression, anger, rebellion, fear, anxiety, increasing inability to recognize one's own faults and a growing dominance of aggressive tendencies.

Guilt not only causes inner turmoil, but it also can eat away and destroy a relationship. In his article, "Sex Before Marriage — Why Should We Wait?", Jerry Evans says, "Sex tends to break up established relationships because of the guilt it produces. . . the greater the pressure to get involved physically, the greater the guilt when you do."[4]

Ron, a manager of a large company, was trying to help his friend Tommy who had been in Ron's youth group years ago. As a high school student, Tommy had been enthusiastic for the Lord. Although he was shy, Tommy had summoned up enough courage to ask Cynthia, a member of the group, for a date. This started a relationship that slowly became more physical and sexual. After high school, they started sleeping together. Although both were Christians, their guilt was washed over by romantic passion. Tommy moved into Cynthia's apartment. They lived together for three years, thinking their love was strong enough to handle any problems. But their arguments became more frequent as they tried to maintain separate identities.

"Last month," Ron said, "Tommy and Cynthia separated with great anguish and hostility. The guilt and anger had driven Tommy to violence and stifling jealousy. He had threatened Cynthia and had followed her, watching her at a distance with binoculars. God had been dumped out of their lives long ago. Now, Tommy was depressed and refused to come back to God." Ron wants to know how to help Tommy and Cynthia. The infection caused by covered guilt is destroying them both.

2. Loss of Self-esteem

Closely tied to guilt is the loss of self-esteem that results from going against both our conscience and God's principles. This is due to a sense of shame that is felt. Self-esteem is the most important aspect governing a person's behavior, particularly with other people. Positive self-esteem is the basic element in the health of any person's personality. Loss of self- esteem can have a long-lasting and widespread effect on a person's life.

Michael had been dating Karen, whom he felt he really loved. Although they were Christians, they allowed their relationship to become more sexually oriented. In the beginning, their sexual experience seemed so right and, for a long time, was emotionally fulfilling. They continued to be involved in their Christian activities, feeling only a small amount of hypocrisy.

But the time came when, like a crack in the wall of a dam, feelings of guilt, shame and immense self-disgust flooded their lives and relationship. Michael felt worthless; he wondered whether he would ever feel good about himself again. Slowly, his relationship with Karen disintegrated. They had glimpsed the depths possible in a sexual relationship, yet, because it was outside the boundaries of marriage and God's will, the fulfillment they felt was only temporary. Eventually, their great experience of love became an inner nightmare. Their sense of well-being — of self-esteem — was destroyed.

Since then, Michael has asked and received God's forgiveness for his sexual sin. But it took several years for him to get over the shame that hung on and to begin to see himself as clean again in God's eyes.

In premarital sexual relations, it is easy to use the other person to meet one's own physical desires. Many times the realization that you are not ultimately concerned for the other person's well being, produces feelings of self-disgust. This, in turn, causes a loss of self-esteem.

3. Flashbacks

Memories have a habit of exploding into the forefront of our minds at the most unlikely moments. Flashbacks of a previous partner or partners remind a person of a painful, broken relationship in the past in which the person had given himself or herself totally. These memories detract from the present relationship.

Psychologists tell us that flashbacks can be a sign of unresolved guilt about past activities. When guilt is suppressed, flashbacks may come back to your conscious mind as mental windows into your personal history. Often they are triggered by thoughts and circumstances that are similar in nature.

Jack, a close friend of mine, has been married for five years. He told me that he has been going through a difficult time in his relationship with his wife. Many times when he is in bed with her, his mind is cluttered with thoughts of other women with whom he was once involved. These flashbacks have made it difficult for him to fully enjoy his wife.

4. Mental Pollution

From puberty on, we all experience sexual desires and fantasies. Added to this, the subject of sex dominates our society so much that it's hard to keep a pure mind as we go about our everyday lives. Entering a sexual relationship further increases the time these desires are a major drive in our lives. The actual fulfillment of intercourse lasts but a short time compared to the amount of time a sexually-active person thinks about and physically feels the desire for another sexual encounter.

Once a relationship is over, a person's mind tends to be even more preoccupied with sex. The heat in the furnace has been turned up and it takes a long time for it to cool down again. It is disturbing to fight aroused and unfulfilled sexual desires continually when you would like to put these behind you. This is true even for many Christians who have confessed a wrong relationship to God and who want to have a clean, pure mind again.

5. Sexual Inhibition

A somewhat opposite phenomenon has recently been named "inhibited sexual desire" or "ISD" by psychologists. The more well-known names for this are frigidity and impotence.

A recent issue of *Time* magazine featured a cover story entitled, "The Revolution Is Over." According to the story, the sexual revolution is no more. Today, ISD, frigidity and impotence account for almost half the case loads of sexual therapists. A well known therapist said that the sexual revolution had resulted in elimination of all taboos, and in satiation and boredom. Since the excitement value of the average sexual practice had been so severely diminished, ISD was now a major problem.[5]

Confirming this, *Psychology Today* surveyed twelve thousand people and found that 28 percent of the men and 40 percent of the women no longer had a desire for sex. For a growing number of people, over-indulgence in sex had deadened sexual desire.[6] A number of years ago, a popular song asked the stinging question, "Is that all there is?" Many people today are asking this question about their sexual involvements.

Relational Consequences

1. Break-Up

Dr. Robert Blood, Jr., author of the standard work, *Marriage*, says, "Intimacy (sexual) produces more broken relationships than strengthened ones. More engagements were broken (in the Burgess and Wallins study) by couples who had intercourse than by those who did not. . . and the more frequent the intercourse, the larger the proportion of rings returned."[7]

As already mentioned, sex tends to break up relationships because of guilt. But break-ups also occur because the foundation of the relationship was built on sexual attraction. This gave a false sense of intimacy, an illusion of what true intimacy is made of. Jerry Evans says that sex lessens our ability to build a relationship in other areas because it gives a feeling of closeness with little effort, so that we neglect developing the other levels of closeness that take more time.[8]

Unmarried couples living together or in trial marriages do not have a good foundation for true intimacy, either. Dr. E. Mansell Pattison of the Medical College of Georgia, says, "My observations lead me to conclude that. . . there is a paradox — a happy union living together, but an unhappy union as soon as they marry. Sexual dissatisfaction is the leading reported cause of the break up."[9]

In many cases, the seeds of divorce are planted long before marriage. Premarital sex is often the real reason for divorce. The violation of integrity and morality that the premarital sex represents is never forgotten. Before marriage, sex may smother a couple's incompatibilities. In marriage, these irreconcilable differences, aggravated by a sense of mistrust, must be faced and so destroy the relationship.

2. Mistrust

Premarital sex may drive a couple apart. Without a lifetime commitment to one another, subtle but real insecurities and suspicions eat away at the relationship. It comes out in questioning thoughts of, "Am I the only one?" or "Will I be dropped for someone else?"

This lack of security may be carried over into marriage. If a person did not wait until marriage to have sex, there's no guarantee that making the relationship legal will change a person's character or habits. Even though the partner promises faithfulness in marriage, will he or she want or be able to withstand the attraction of other sexual encounters when a mate is ill or away?

If you can't trust the other person or yourself before marriage, it may be even more difficult after the wedding. It is known that a high percentage of those who engage in premarital sex often become involved in extra-marital affairs. Sexual habits do not die easily.

Mistrust also breeds possessiveness. With physical closeness comes emotional dependency. Like it or not, this is true, even in a casual affair. If you can't trust the other person and have made an emotional investment in that person, you become more and more possessive. Afraid of losing your emotional investment, you try to control your partner's activities.

When I was a pastoral counselor, a couple on the brink of divorce came to see me. Steve was a well-to-do insurance man. Janice was his second wife. During Steve's previous marriage, he and Janice had become involved while she was his secretary. Moments of innocent flirtation in the office gradually led to physical intimacy. He divorced his first wife and married Janice.

When I saw them, Janice was staying at home taking care of their child. But she kept remembering what they used to do when she was Steve's secretary. Now she distrusts Steve and fears that he might be involved with his present secretary or other female employees. Janice is becoming more and more possessive. Constantly, Janice wonders where Steve is and what he is doing. Their arguments have mushroomed. A deep root of bitterness has caused their marriage to deteriorate.

3. Comparison

It's a natural tendency to compare the present with the past and a present relationship to a past one. The more intimate the love-making and the more partners one has had, the greater will be the tendency to compare a new person to others. Your own comparisons and the fear of your partner's comparing you to others can make technique and performance the center of attention in your love-making. You become more interested in being good at a particular sexual activity than in developing commitment and communication between the two of you.

Comparison in any area of a relationship can undermine it but comparison in the physical area can devastate it. Focus is put on what you can get, rather than on what you can give. If you feel disappointment in love- making, you may withdraw from the person, unless you are already committed to developing total life intimacy. You may feel discouraged if your present partner doesn't display the kind of sexual reactions you have come to expect from previous experiences.

Physical Consequences

Physical repercussions of sex outside marriage, such as venereal disease and pregnancy, affect millions of people. I have discovered some people who find comfort in statistics as always referring to other people, not to themselves. "I'm different," they say. "It won't happen to me." Yet, I have personally counseled hundreds who have had venereal disease happen to them — always unexpectedly.

1. Herpes

About one of every ten adults in America is afflicted with genital herpes, the most prevalent venereal disease today. Infections are characterized by fever, swollen lymph nodes and numerous clusters of painful vesicles all on or near the genitals. These often develop into shallow ulcerations. They take two weeks to heal but reoccur periodically. Although a drug is now available to reduce some of the pain and frequency of the disease, there is no cure yet for herpes.[10]

2. Gonorrhea

Until recently, gonorrhea was the most frequently reported communicable disease in the United States. From 1976 to 1984, the prevalence of gonorrhea increased dramatically. The disease affects the epididymis, prostate and seminal vesicles in men. In some cases, it infects the pharynx. In women, it can cause dysuria, urethral or vaginal discharge and frequently leads to inflammation of the Fallopian tubes with subsequent damage and/or blockage. The problem is further complicated by the emergence of strains of gonorrhea resistant to penicillin and other antibiotics. More than five percent of males affected show no symptoms of their venereal disease.[11] However, they are carriers and can pass the infection to their partners.

3. Syphillis

In 1984 there were 69,888 new cases of syphillis reported. This includes those in the primary, secondary and latent stages of the disease."[12] The disease starts as a painless bump or chancre sore. But within weeks, the person develops symptoms such as headaches, sore throats, enlarged lymph nodes, joint aches and pain, weight loss and a generalized skin rash. The infection then goes into a latent stage, without symptoms, that can later flare up and cause serious disease to the central nervous system or heart.

4. Chlamydia

According to the Centers for Disease Control in Atlanta, Georgia, chlamydia is now estimated to be the most frequently reported communicable disease in America. This bacteria, which can severely damage the tubes, has now become a leading cause of infertility. Between three and four million new cases of chlamydia are reported each year. Often women are unaware of the symptoms and may not find out they have it until years later when they are discovered to be infertile. A number of researchers have found an association between the use of oral contraceptives in adolescents and chlamydia infections. The exact reason for this is not known.[13] It may be just reflecting the increased sexual exposure of teen-aged pill users. In men chlamydia causes an enlarged and tender prostate, inflammation of the urethra and infection of the urinary tract. It is also responsible for conjunctival infection, respiratory tract colonization and pneumonia in newborns and infants.

Dr. Khatamee, an Associate Clinical Professor of Obstetrics and Gynecology of the New York University School of Medicine, says, "The pill, the IUD and the diaphragm have all produced a tremendous sense of sexual freedom. But what we don't adequately teach our young people when dispensing these birth control methods is that, although they are protecting themselves from unwanted pregnancy, they are exposing themselves to a variety of infectious agents that can threaten their future fertility."[14]

5. Acquired Immune Deficiency Syndrome (AIDS)

At one time, AIDS was believed to be limited to the homosexual community and to blood transfusion patients. Now it has spread to the heterosexual community through bisexual males' activities with female prostitutes, who then pass the virus on to heterosexual males. Not only do people with the active AIDS virus pass on the disease, but so do inactive carriers of the virus who develop no symptoms. Of the estimated 300,000 to 500,000 people who have been exposed to the virus, 10 to 20 percent will develop the disease. Once contracted, the disease is virtually always fatal.

AIDS represents a wide range of clinical abnormalities, from severe infections and unusual cancerous process to milder ones whose only symptoms are swollen glands, fever, and loss of weight. Besides the blood stream, the virus has been found in the nervous system and the brain. The AIDS-causing virus, HLTV-3, destroys the immune system. No cure is available. If a vaccine is developed, it is projected that it would not be available until at least 1990.

6. Pelvic Inflammatory Disease (PID)

Salpingitis, commonly called pelvic inflammatory disease, is an infection of the Fallopian tubes and the surrounding areas or organs. It is usually, but not always, caused by gonorrhea. With this disease, a woman experiences severe abdominal pain, fever, and cervical discharge. Complications may include tubal abscess, infertility and ectopic pregnancy. If the abscess ruptures into the body cavity, it is a surgical emergency and death may quickly follow. Every year, one million American women are treated for PID.[15]

How can a woman prevent this traumatic disease? Dr. Hager, Associate Clinical Professor, Department of Obstetrics and Gynecology, University of Kentucky College of Medicine, has said it simply. "Women who are not sexually active do not get PID."[16]

7. Genital Cancer

McCalls Magazine surveyed over one thousand doctors, 80 percent of whom reported an increase in the number of patients with gynecological problems due to increased sexual activity, sexual activity at a younger age, and multiple sexual partners.[17]

"If liberal sexual lifestyles continue," predicts gynecologist-oncologist Dr. J. Max Austin, Jr., "an epidemic of cervical cancer among women is likely to occur. Young women who have had three or more sexual partners are at a much greater than average risk for having a dysplasia (a precancerous condition) of the cervix."[18]

Dr. Ralph Richart, Columbia University College of Physicians and Surgeons, states:

Condyloma viral infection is widely prevalent among sexually active women under 30 and the risk increases with the number of sexual partners, or if the male partner has had multiple partners. Women who have condylomas are between 1,500 and 2,000 times at greater risk of developing cervical cancer than those who do not. High risk status can be conferred on a woman if she has early intercourse defined as before age 20, multiple sex partners, or has a sole partner who has had multiple sexual partners.[19]

Dr. Richart summarizes his conclusions by saying, "A woman who has a monogamous union with a man who is monogamous has zero risk of cervical cancer."[20]

8. Ectopic Pregnancies

Experts say that ectopic pregnancies (pregnancies that implant outside the uterus and most often in the Fallopian tubes) have reached epidemic proportions. From 1970 to 1980 the rate increased by more than 200 percent.[21] During that same time period, the number of hospitalizations for ectopic pregnancies nearly tripled.[22] Since then, it has continued to increase even more. The rise is attributed to the increasing incidence of sexually transmitted diseases.[23]

Because VD and PID sear the Fallopian tubes, the fertilized egg is prevented from lodging in the uterus. The resultant ectopic pregnancy causes serious complications. Dr. Dorfman of Mount Sinai Medical Center reports that this kind of pregnancy "carries a relative death risk about ten times greater than that of a legal induced abortion and more than fifty times greater than that of a childbirth."[24] In addition, there is a 50 percent infertility rate after ectopic pregnancy."[25]

9. Other Effects

Medical experts are now discovering that sexually transmitted diseases (STDs) have a variety of other effects on the body. Dr. Michael Heller, Director of the House Staff Teaching Program, Emergency Medicine Department of Franklin Square Hospital, Baltimore, writes, "It is now known that STDs can affect every organ system."[26] The list of problems includes: tendonitis, arthritis, urethritis, hepatitis, abdominal pain, gastrointestinal infections, AIDS, aseptic meningitis, eye infections and cervical cancer.[27]

Dr Heller concluded, "Diseases caused by sexual practices can affect virtually any body function, while the genital region may be clinically uninvolved. The known manifestations of STDs are increasing."[28]

As you can see, in the physical area, the consequences of playing around with sex are overwhelming.

Social Consequences

Most people don't want to hurt anyone, themselves or another person, when they have sex. They just want to experience some pleasure and closeness with someone else. But an hour of sexual pleasure can bring a lifetime, even generations of hurt and agony.

The social repercussions of sex outside marriage not only affect the couple, but their sexual behavior can end up affecting many others as well.

1. Unwanted Pregnancies

We all know that there are no foolproof contraceptives. Despite their use, unwanted pregnancies do occur. The two people most affected are the woman and the child. Not only does a woman have an unwanted baby living inside her, but the situation often causes tremendous social upheaval in her family. Family ties are severely strained as family members come to terms with what has happened. Then, if the child is allowed to be born and grow, the child's life is vastly affected.

2. Abortion

Many unwanted babies grow up and are able to overcome the obstacles of their beginnings. Many more are having their lives snuffed out, before they are given a chance to be born, by the very people responsible for their existence — their mothers — who tragically realize the hardships that a baby would give them when all they really wanted was a little pleasure.

3. Cultural Disintegration

A famous saying tells us, "The only thing we learn from history is that we don't learn from history." Time and again, when the moral fiber of a nation has deteriorated, a fall has followed.

Anthropologist J. D. Unwin made an exhaustive study of more than eighty primitive and advanced civilizations. Each culture reflected a similar pattern. Those civilizations with strict sexual codes made the greatest cultural progress. Every society that extended sexual permissiveness to its people soon perished. Professor Unwin said there were no exceptions to this rule.[29]

William Stephen, another anthropologist, found that out of ninety primitive cultures, those with the greatest sexual freedom made the poorest cultural record.[30]

A society begins to crumble from within when it is characterized by sexual permissiveness, a disintegration of the moral fiber, and a failure to follow biblical concepts of morality. Psychologist James Dobson says, "Mankind has known intuitively for at least fifty centuries that indiscriminate sexual activity represents both an individual and a corporate threat to survival. And history bears it out."[31]

According to the book, *Sex and the Christian Marriage*, around 30 percent of the women in the early 1950s had premarital intercourse. In the 1970s, over two-thirds had experienced sex before marriage. An encouraging note, however, is that in the mid-1980s, the increase in sexual knowledge and the growing conservatism in America had brought about a corresponding decrease in premarital sex.[32]

Singles need to weigh not only personal considerations when choosing their sexual behavior but also how their actions affect society — the smaller society of people they know well, and also that of their entire culture. In the Book of Genesis, Cain questioned God by saying, "Am I my brother's keeper?" God's answer has always been yes.

Spiritual Consequences

Of all the negative results of immoral sex, the spiritual consequences are the most severe. They eat away at the soul like a cancer and produce results that last through all eternity. People may be concerned about the physical and relational aspects of their sexual actions because these hurt so much and create concern and worry. But they should have the same reactions to the spiritual ramifications. However, responses to spiritual consequences range from apathy to short-lived desires for change that produce tears with little genuine action. Such responses are further evidence of the devastating spiritual consequences of immoral sex.

1. Coldness Toward God

Sin is defined in the Bible as a deviation from the ways of God; it is the missing of the mark of God's righteousness, a transgression of God's law. In Romans 6:23, we are told, "The wages (results) of sin is death." Death here refers not only to eternal separation from God, as terrible as that is, but to coldness toward God here and now. A person loses the excitement and joy of being a Christian. It becomes harder to read the Bible because it is a reminder of what that person's life should be. Prayer becomes less frequent unless a problem arises; then begging and pleading erupts from a hardened heart.

After his extra-marital sex with Bathsheba, David hid from God for one year. In Psalm 32:3 and 4 he describes his agony: "When I kept silent about my sin, my body wasted away through my groaning all day long. For day and night (God's) hand was heavy upon me; my vitality was drained away as with the fever-heat of summer."

The person who hides from God is robbed of all the benefits of a close relationship with Him.

2. Coldness Toward Faithful Christians

When we walk in darkness, we don't want to be around people who walk in the light. They remind us of the joy that we no longer possess. Who wants to sing enthusiastically about a righteous God when there is little righteousness inside the heart?

Some people, of course, get around this difficulty by going to Christian meetings, using Christian phrases, smiling at appropriate times during a Christian message and singing the songs. But these people are empty of spiritual life. They have the appearance of Christianity but they are dead inside. The Bible calls them hypocrites. They become critical of others who enjoy the Lord, but they have little personal interest in true dedication and faith. They simply put in their time, but their hearts are like stone.

3. Misery

When one is running from God, misery will catch up with that person eventually. Then the person searches for someone to turn to.

That's what had happened when Julie wrote me a letter. She had heard me speak at a singles convention. Her story is a sad one.

"I met Jesus Christ when I was twelve years old. My spiritual life had several ups and downs, but now I'm in the deepest down. I don't remember my last faithful prayer or the last time I opened my Bible. I feel miserable. To be more accurate, my spirit is miserable.

"A long time ago I used to be a very strong believer and my life was full of joy. I was dependent on the Lord for almost everything. Now my life has deteriorated, spiritually and morally.

"It began when I met Neil, a very attractive man. I knew that he was not for me since he was not a Christian. My stubbornness was great, however, so I started dating him and fell in love. I fooled myself by thinking that I was going to make him a Christian. The opposite has happened.

"At first I refused his sexual advances but I was weak and lonely. Instead of getting closer to God, I got closer to Neil. Little by little, he started touching me more sexually. I let him because I needed someone physically and emotionally close to me. Finally, we made love. Now we do it often.

"I am sinning. I don't know what to do. I love Neil very, very much but I want to come back to God. I know I should break up with Neil but I can't. It seems like I can't live without him.

"I can't love people any more. I can't forgive. I can't stop lying. I can't read the Bible. I just can't be a Christian any more.

"Please help me. I am desperate. I want to come back to God, but I can't help feeling I will fail again as has happened so many times. I can't leave Neil. I love him. What if I leave Neil and can't come back to God? I may never be able to come back to God if you don't help me."

What a sad situation. My heart reached out to Julie in her confusion. She can come back to God. God will forgive her, but it will mean giving up everything — including Neil and her desires — in order that her needs might be filled by no one but God.

I wrote Julie a long letter, encouraging her and counseling her toward the way back. Much of that information is given in the next chapter.

God was thinking of our welfare when He commanded us to "abstain from sexual immorality" (1 Thessalonians 4:3). For those who haven't, He still is thinking of their welfare and offers a way back. Healing can come, but how much better if the painful wounds had never occurred in the first place. Saying yes and being sorry can involve much more than we ever bargained for.

---

1. Why would guilt tend to eat away an established relationship?

2. What would keep you from becoming sexually involved with someone outside of marriage?

3. How does God view a person who has been involved in a sexual relationship outside of marriage?

Chapter Six
Expect Only Time to Heal

"I remember standing in the ocean one day," a friend once told me, "calling to someone on the beach. Suddenly, an unexpected wave came crashing over me. I found myself being swept under the water and dragged along the ocean floor with the sand biting into my hands and face."

Sometimes our past and even our present sneaks up behind us like that wave and crashes down on us; this upsets our emotional balance and sweeps us to the bottom in depression. Memories of loss, failure and guilt bite into our emotions and inflame past wounds with as much sting as ever.

Almost all of us have emotional scars of one kind or another — painful memories of broken promises, a broken heart or even a broken life. We trust someone with our heart, our deepest secrets or our life, only to find the person untrustworthy. We open ourselves up only to be shut out. Sometimes we feel the shame and feeling of worthlessness that come from the memory of using or hurting someone else. Whether the blame is primarily ours or another person's, the relationship is over and there is the feeling of being empty, bitter, foolish and alone.

To give oneself emotionally to another and to be cut off brings deep wounds. But to give of oneself completely — body, soul, and spirit — and then to be abandoned can bring total devastation.

In his book, *Healing For Damaged Emotions*, David Seamands says, "Sex, being what it is, can produce the deadliest of all emotional conflicts: dread and desire, fear and pleasure, love and hate, all combined into a violent emotional earthquake which can tear a person's guts out."[1] The physical adds a dimension which makes the cut go much deeper.

As I counsel with singles all over the U. S., I come across thousands of wounded people, both Christians and non-Christians. I have found that a large percentage of them are experiencing an "emotional earthquake" within because they became involved sexually with someone outside of marriage. Many of the people I've counseled have given themselves to someone completely only to have their dreams shattered; in the process they find themselves shattered inwardly as well.

As one person wrote:

> Time passes. I wait for the pain to subside. I thought time heals. When? That's the question. How long? How long till this lump dissolves from my throat. How long till I quit feeling like a hollow body walking around? Till the agony of this whole ordeal goes away? Till I forget how much I love and miss the person and yet hate, as well? I feel like I live in eternity, like this hurt will go on endlessly. Please, Time, heal me!

Time heals all wounds, so we've heard. Yet, in reality, time by itself only dulls the pain or forms a scab over a festering sore. Yes, healing takes time, but healing also takes more than time.

Healing Is a Process

As mentioned earlier, today's generation wants instant gratification. This carries over into the area of healing as well. We want our wounds healed now! We want everything to be okay now. We want quick fixes and easy answers. However, when it comes to having emotional wounds healed, there are answers but they aren't always easy ones. The process of healing takes many steps.

Step 1: Realize that time plus effort are involved.

The first step toward the healing process is to recognize that there are no quick cures. It is foolish to think we can rush the healing process in a physical wound. It is equally as foolish to think we can rush the healing process in an emotional wound. If we try to rush this process, we are likely to end up with only a superficial covering over the wound.

Although we need to allow time to work its cures, we can't passively wait for time alone to accomplish healing. We have an active part to play in the healing process ourselves. Otherwise, we have an uncleaned and uncared for wound which may or may not heal over. If it does form a scar, it will be sensitive to the touch and may involve a festering sore underneath that eventually spreads poison through the rest of the body. Taking action to help the healing of an emotional wound is as important as it is for a physical wound.

Step 2: Desire to be healed.

Next, we need to answer the question, "Do I really want to see healing in my life?" Jesus asked a man who had been an invalid for thirty-eight years this same question. (John 5:5-9) Why? One reason was to test the man's own desire for healing. Jesus put into the man's hands the power of healing, dependent on how much the man desired healing.

Why wouldn't someone want to be healed? It could be because of the benefits found in being afflicted. A person can become so accustomed to coping with the disadvantages of afflictions that those disadvantages eventually seem comfortable, even desirable.

For instance, the blind beggar in the Bible was totally dependent on others. His life was simple, uncomplicated. If he was healed, it meant becoming responsible for his own financial survival. He would have to learn to work at a trade, not sit and beg all day. His excuses for not leading a more productive life would no longer be valid. People would no longer be willing to help him. Healing would mean a drastic change in his lifestyle.

Sometimes, it is easier to cling to emotional wounds, whether they are deserved (the consequences of past sins) or undeserved, than to face the feelings that are the result of wounding experiences.

Some people fear that facing their true feelings will be too much to handle. Others would rather believe that present misery is deserved payment for past sins, than be willing to accept God's forgiveness and then to forgive themselves. Some withhold forgiveness by nursing a grudge, in order to make the other person keep on paying for his or her sin. Sometimes we become so used to living with hurt and pain that we are afraid to live without it. If healed from an emotional wound, there would no longer be excuses to keep from being more responsible and productive in life.

Therefore, before you go on to the next step in the healing process, it is important to ask yourself, "Do I truly want to be healed?"

If your answer is yes, then you'll face these important steps: asking Jesus to help in the healing process, facing and releasing emotions, receiving God's forgiveness, gaining God's perspective on your wounds, forgiving yourselves and forgiving others.

Step 3: Allow Jesus to help in the healing.

Realize that you need Jesus to go through the healing process with you. The prophet Isaiah describes Jesus' healing abilities in this way:

He was despised and rejected by men,
A man of sorrows, and familiar with suffering;
Like one from whom men hide their faces,
He was despised, and we esteemed Him not.
Surely He took up our infirmities,
And carried our sorrows....
But He was pierced for our transgressions,
He was crushed for our iniquities;
The punishment that brought us peace was upon Him,
And by His wounds we are healed (Isaiah 53:3-5 NIV).

Here we see a Savior who not only took on the punishment for our sin, but also took on a total identification with our wounds and pain. As a result, Jesus has been called the "Wounded Healer."

More than anyone, Jesus sees and understands the depth of our pain and sorrow. He is with us with an open heart and open arms, throughout the entire process of healing (Hebrews 4:15,16). David Seamands says, "There is nothing you can share out of the agonizing hurts and depths and hates and rages of your soul that God has not heard. There is nothing you take to Him that He will not understand. He will receive you with love and grace."

Jesus understands that the way of healing is not easy. Some of the steps can be agonizing. He knows we may fail and falter along the road of our healing. Yet He is with us, coaxing us through His Holy Spirit — the great Comforter — to keep moving ahead. And Jesus is as pleased with us during the healing process, even in our failures and falterings, as is a parent whose child is going through a growing process like learning to walk.

When my daughter, Rachel, was learning to walk, we were excited when she took three or four little steps before falling down on her bottom. We were just as pleased with her after she had fallen as we were while she was taking those first small steps, even though she cried out of pain and frustration from the fall.

When I saw Rachel fall, I didn't say, "When is this kid ever going to learn to walk? What a failure! All she has to do is put one foot in front of the other! It's so easy!"

Instead, I would smile, because I loved her so much; I knew that walking was a learning process and falling was part of that process. Gradually, Rachel walked farther between falls. We would pick her up, steady her on her feet and cheer her on as she tried again. I love watching my daughter grow and overcome barriers.

In much the same way, God views and understands the process of physical and emotional healing. He created healing. He is pleased with us during each step of that process because He loves watching us overcome the emotional and spiritual barriers in our lives. The Wounded Healer is with us and helps us as we step out and walk through the healing process.

Step 4: Face and release your emotions.

Chuck Swindoll, in his book, *Starting Over*, has said, "To start over, you have to know where you are. To get somewhere else, it's necessary to know where you're presently standing."[3] To move on and see true healing take place in our lives, we need to find out where we stand with our emotions. We need to identify our hidden feelings. By facing our emotions, owning up to the worst, we rob those feelings of having the power to keep on hurting us.

We cannot erase the past, but the pain and wreckage that is left can be healed as we face and release our emotions.

In *Feelings, Where They Come From and How To Handle Them*, Joan Jacobs says we try to close up the wound "because we don't know what to do with our emotional cancers. We treat our feelings as we do persistent children when we're busy. We try to shake them off or shush them up."[4]

When we try to "shush up" our feelings, we stop the healing process, as well as our ability to give and receive forgiveness. Sometimes people think they have their negative feelings under control when they've only buried them alive. But these negative feelings constantly climb out of that grave.

We cannot put the past behind us as long as there are uncried tears that need to be shed and half-felt feelings that need to be experienced. We cannot fully experience God's forgiveness, forgive ourselves or forgive others until we first face the pain.

In his book on forgiveness, Lewis Smedes made these observations:

> You find freedom to forgive when you let yourself feel the pain you want to forgive them for.... There is no real forgiving unless there is first relentless exposure and honest judgment. When we forgive evil we do not excuse it, we do not tolerate it, we do not smother it. We look the evil full in the face, call it what it is, let its horror shock and stun and enrage us and only then do we forgive it.[5]

When we are too afraid to own up to our pain — anger, hurt, shame, or guilt — and won't permit ourselves to feel it fully, we dodge the real issue of forgiveness. As Lewis Smedes also says, "Forgetting, in fact, may be a dangerous way to escape the inner surgery of the heart that we call forgiving."[6]

We need to face feelings and problems with ruthless honesty, and, with God's grace, come to grips with the feelings that keep us bound and crippled. We must ask God to help us get in touch with our feelings and to take responsibility for them; then we must ask God to release us from their power.

In a real sense, we need to relive the emotions of the experiences that have hurt us. Then we need to express those emotions out loud or in writing. While expressing this anger, hurt, shame or guilt, visualize and know that the Lord's presence is with you. Keep on expressing these thoughts, feelings and tears until you have nothing more to express. How long this will take will depend upon the depth of the wound. Remember that the Lord will not be surprised or afraid of the wording of our emotions for He knows our deepest thoughts already. We can feel free to open up the flood gates to Him.

Sometimes this expressing of our emotions should be done to a faithful, trustworthy friend — someone to whom we can pour out our hearts. This needs to be someone who will accept us in spite of our emotions and who will help us go through them. Confessing our emotions and sin with such a friend is like seeing God's love with skin on. In James 5:16 the Lord encourages us to confess to others: "Therefore confess your sins to one another and pray for one another, so that you may be healed."

Step 5: Receive God's forgiveness.

Before we can forgive ourselves or others fully, we must first experience God's forgiveness. His forgiveness can free us from the sin and hurt that entangle us and keep us chained to our past.

Erwin Lutzer says, "Many Christians are handcuffed by regret. By nature, we know that sin has to be paid for. Consequently, some people nurse their regrets and cling to their grief. The reason? They believe that such an attitude is necessary to punish themselves. Unconsciously, they want to pay for their sins."[7]

We don't need to pay for our own sins, nor does God want us to. By His death and sacrifice on the cross, Jesus Christ paid, not just for some of our sin, but for all of our sin. Our sin — past, present, and future — is covered under Christ's blood shed on the cross (Hebrews 10:10-18).

On the day of Christ's death, He cried out from the cross, "It is finished" (John 19:30). This statement expresses an extremely significant concept in regard to our forgiveness. In Greek, the word is used primarily for business transactions. When this Greek word, translated "it is finished," was written across a bill, it meant "paid in full." Christ was saying, by the act of dying on the cross, that our bill or debt of sin was paid in full. Therefore, we never need to pay for or make up for our sins. It is already finished, paid in full.

Because the price of His forgiveness has already been paid, God does not find it difficult to forgive us. We can come to Him no matter what we've done or who we are. God accepts us fully and forgives us completely. All we need to do is to accept that forgiveness freely.

Many of us, including Christians, will view God as a stern debt collector, unless we realize what God accomplished on the cross. Without that realization, we miss the whole reason for His coming to earth. Jesus said, "It is not those who are healthy who need a physician, but those who are sick. I did not come to call the righteous, but sinners" (Mark 2:17). If you have failed miserably in love relationships, or in any way, then you are the reason why Jesus came. Remember, He came willingly because He loves you and me so very much.

To be forgiven by God recreates our past in the sense that His forgiveness washes us whiter than snow and lets us stand clean before Him. As we accept God's forgiveness, we can begin to experience freedom from our past. For those who have known physical intimacies that should have been reserved for a marriage partner, God restores emotional virginity as His forgiveness is accepted and His healing process experienced.

As we begin to accept and receive God's forgiveness, we begin also to take part in the next step of the healing process.

Step 6: Gain God's perspective on your wounds.

An extremely important part of healing is to recognize that God has the ability to take our hurts and failures and turn them to our good and to His glory. It is amazing, but God can work all things together for our good. Romans 8:28 says, "And we know that God causes all things to work together for good to those who love God, to those who are called according to His purpose." This doesn't mean that all things are good in themselves or that we escape the natural consequences of our actions. It does mean that God somehow takes all the actions and reactions of our lives, good and bad, and works them together for our ultimate good.

David Seamands, in the book *Healing For Damaged Emotions,* has some great comments on this concept:

Total healing is more than soothing painful memories, more than forgiving and being forgiven of harmful resentments, even more than the reprogramming of our minds. Healing is the miracle of God's recycling grace, where He takes it all and makes good come out of it, where He actually recycles our hangups into wholeness and usefulness.... God does not change the actual, factual nature of the evil which occurs. Humanly speaking, nothing can change this; it is still evil, tragic, senseless, and perhaps unjust and absurd. But God can change the meaning of it for your total life. God can weave it into the design and purpose of your life, so that it all lies within the circle of His redeeming and recycling activity.[8]

As you look at past relationships or whatever it is that has left emotional wounds, ask God to show you ways that He might use these in your life for good. We don't have to continue to live in despair or guilt. In God, we can have true hope and can move forward to be used by Him to help others.

Before Simon Peter betrayed Him, Jesus said, "Simon, Simon, Satan has demanded permission to sift you as wheat. But I have prayed for you, that your faith may not fail. And you, when once you have turned again, strengthen your brothers" (Luke 22:31,32). Jesus knew Peter was going to turn against Him. But Christ knew that this betrayal could be used ultimately for good in Peter's life and in the lives of others.

Our lives may be a scrap pile, but God can build trophies from scrap piles. To gain God's perspective on your wounds, keep an eye out for how He has used or can use your pain and failures and wounds for good.

Step 7: Forgive yourself.

Taking the step to forgive yourself can be very difficult, especially if you see your wounds as self-inflicted. Forgiving yourself, however, is essential if you are to see healing. When you forgive yourself, you become both the forgiver and the forgiven.

If we do not forgive ourselves, then we haven't truly accepted God's forgiveness in our hearts. And if we can't forgive ourselves, we will find it difficult to forgive others. Refusing to forgive ourselves leaves us open and vulnerable to attacks from Satan.

In his classic satire, *The Screwtape Letters*,[9] C. S. Lewis describes Satan's plan to get Christians preoccupied with their failures. When Satan does this, he wins the battle. Why? Because the more we turn inward, concentrating on self (even on self's failures), the more we are alienated from God, from our true selves and from others. An unforgiving spirit directed at self or at others grows like a thorn bush in our hearts.

When we forgive ourselves we must be honest with ourselves. It has been said that forgiving is for realists. Simply pushing failures or sin out of our minds is not forgiveness.

We can go to one of two extremes: either whipping ourselves over and over, or minimizing what we've done. Neither of these options helps to bring about healing.

When we forgive ourselves, we must look at self and our sin honestly, accept God's forgiveness for that sin, ask Him to give us some insight on our inner makeup and needs and then make a clear-cut decision to forgive ourselves. Although forgiveness of self should be definite, we may find that we need to remind ourselves of that forgiveness daily until the past no longer brings painful memories to mind.

Step 8: Forgive others.

To complete the process of healing, we need to forgive the person or persons who played a part in bringing hurt and pain into our lives. Until we go through most of the other steps, however, it may be very difficult to even consider forgiving the person who wounded us.

Forgiving someone else does not change the other person. Forgiving others changes us. It frees us from the past and from our need to try to seek revenge, either actively or mentally. If we don't forgive that other person, our minds will be stuck in a "get even" channel. Something like a videotape inside our minds will continue to replay the painful incident, not with what actually happened, but with what we would have liked to have said or done diffrently. This keeps us hooked into the hate and the pain. Forgiveness turns off this mental replay and releases us from the channel of painful memories that keeps our wounds open and festering.

Hidden hate and anger not only affect us but, sooner or later, they also affect our other relationships. An unforgiving spirit eventually produces bitterness toward anything that vaguely reminds us of the painful experience. This spills over, sometimes subtly and sometimes obviously, into our other relationships, even with those we love. In the end bitterness, not the pain and hurt, will destroy us.

How then do we forgive another person? See your own forgiveness before God. Through Christ's forgiveness we have had a tremendous debt to God erased. God has released us from having to pay that debt of sin against us. But often we are like the unmerciful servant Jesus talked about in Matthew 18:23-35.

In this parable, Jesus tells about a servant of the king who owed the king ten thousand talents (worth more than several million dollars today). To settle the account, the king was going to sell the man, his family and all his possessions. When the man fell on his knees and begged for more time to repay the debt, the king responded with compassion and cancelled out his debt entirely. This part of the story can be likened to the debt of sin that we owed God.

But what did the former debtor do then? "But that slave went out, he found one of his fellow-slaves who owed him a hundred denarii [a few dollars]. He seized him and began to choke him saying 'Pay back what you owe!' So His fellow-slave fell down and began to entreat him, saying, 'Have patience with me, and I will repay you.'" The man refused his own debtor's plea. Instead, he ended up having him thrown in jail.

What a perfect illustration of what we do when we refuse to forgive others after God has completely cancelled out our debt. Any refusal within our hearts to forgive others puts us in the same category as this unmerciful servant.

No matter how much someone has hurt us, it cannot compare with the debt we had with God for our sin. The other person's offense toward us is very small in comparison. God has shown us complete forgiveness and mercy. In light of this, how can we have an unforgiving, unmerciful heart toward those who have sinned against us? Forgiveness of others is not easy, especially if the wound is deep. To forgive completely takes time. But when we get this comparison in perspective, it helps to make the way of forgiveness easier.

While focusing on the pain that someone else has caused us, we need to ask the question, "What did I do to hurt the other person?" Many times we are not totally blameless and pure in a situation. We need to look honestly, not only at what the other person has done to us, but also at what we may have done to that person.

In forgiving another person, it helps to have some understanding of the person and what his or her needs are. If we look beyond the behavior that hurt us and see that person's inner needs, we can begin to see the situation more objectively. This enables us to see the person apart from the wrong they have done to us and makes forgiving them much easier.

You will know you are beginning to forgive someone, when you begin to wish them well and truly want the best for them. It's very difficult to do this when there is bitterness still left inside.

Through forgiving others we can let go of the bitterness and anger that keep us knotted up inside. Only in forgiveness can we find freedom from the pain, the hurt and the misery that can come our way in life.

As we go through the healing process with a former lover, a former friend, a relative or a work colleague, we can begin to see our wounds healed and be freed from the pain of the past. God will take our broken heart, broken life and broken promises and restore us to being whole persons, perhaps more whole than we were before the experience that hurt us. Then He enables us to help bring healing to other people's lives. The God of hope and mercy is in the business of taking broken people and putting them together again.

_____

1. How do you deal with wounds in your life?

2. Why is forgiving ourselves so difficult to do?

3. In what ways can God use a pain, a failure, or a wound you have suffered for ultimate good for you and for others?

Section Two

How to Start and Star
a Friendship

Chapter Seven
Share Total Intimacy

When Stephanie first moved to Chicago it seemed that people were always asking her if she knew Roy. She was lonely and wanted to get to know people. At an office party, she spotted Roy and was attracted to him immediately. She must have been staring at him, because a co-worker asked her, "Do you know Roy?"

"No," Stephanie replied, "but I sure would like to." The girl introduced them and in a few weeks, Roy asked her for a date.

During that first date, she returned from the restaurant ladies' room to find Roy entertaining a group of people with his antics. She was watching with the rest of the crowd when another girl asked her, "Do you know that funny fellow?"

"Yes, a little," Stephanie said, somewhat embarrassed. "He's my date."

Getting to know Roy better became a regular thing. Many dates and a year later, Stephanie and Roy became engaged. They celebrated their engagement at a very nice restaurant overlooking the lake. As usual, she found Roy kibitzing with the people around him when she returned to their table. As she approached, a waitress asked her if she knew the guy who was keeping his end of the restaurant entertained. Used to Roy's antics by then, and no longer flustered by them, she answered, "Oh, I know him pretty well. He's my fiance."

Six months later, at the rehearsal dinner for their wedding, a childhood friend of Roy's started teasing Stephanie. "Do you really know this crazy guy you're marrying?" he said. "If you did, I'm sure you'd think twice about getting yourself tied to this nut!"

Laughing at his teasing, Stephanie said, "You bet I know him. That's why I'm marrying him."

Having been asked the question so many times during their courtship, Stephanie started thinking about it more seriously. Did she really know Roy? Well, if not, she knew she would once they were married.

As the years went by, Stephanie often thought about that question. Did she really know who Roy was? And each year she could say she knew him better than the year before. At the same time, she would always ask herself, "But do I really, truly know him? How long will that take?"

How long? That question can be partially answered by something my dad told me one day. After forty-one years of marriage, my father admitted to me, "Dick, sometimes I still don't understand your mother!"

To know a person takes a lifetime of working at a relationship. Building intimacy doesn't come overnight or even after several months of dating.

A dictionary defines intimacy as: a close personal relationship marked by affection, love, and knowledge of each other's inner character, essential nature, or inmost true self; complete intermixture, compounding and interweaving.

Carl Rubenstein, author of *In Search of Intimacy*, gives this list of defining features: openness, honesty, mutual self-disclosure, caring, warmth, protecting, helping, being devoted, mutually attentive, mutually committed, dropping defenses, becoming emotionally attached and feeling distressed when separation occurs.[1]

The Real Meaning of Intimacy

Over the years the meaning of the word *intimacy* has taken on primarily a sexual connotation. In fact, the secondary meaning of the word, as listed in Webster's Dictionary, says it refers to an illicit sexual affair. So today, if a person says he or she is intimate with someone, most people assume the two have had sexual relations together.

I define true intimacy as total life sharing — sharing your life completely with someone else. It includes being open to and deeply involved in the inner and outer life of another person by seeking to understand all of the aspects that make up that person. Intimacy is a process, not a once- for-all accomplishment. Each of us is developing, growing, learning and aging in all aspects of our lives. Life is in constant flux, so intimacy, if it is in a healthy state, is not static but constantly developing and growing, too.

The Five Areas of Life

The five major areas of life can be defined as the social, emotional, mental, physical, and spiritual. These can be represented by a five-pointed star. Knowing only one or two of these areas of another person's makeup leaves a very lopsided impression of who that person is. To be intimate with someone, we must share

SOCIAL

SPIRITUAL   MENTAL

PHYSICAL   EMOTIONAL

joys and sorrows, ups and downs, likes and dislikes and the strengths and weaknesses in each of these areas. In this way we can know them and be known by them as true people, not as facades or fakes. Through mutual caring, giving and accepting of the person as he or she truly is, we both grow.

In this section, a chapter is devoted to each of these five aspects of life. Practical suggestions are given on how to develop relational intimacy in each aspect.

First of all, to evaluate your knowledge of a person whom you consider an intimate friend, see how well you can answer

"The Intimacy Quiz." Grade yourself on a scale of one to five. One is a definite no, three is a neutral (somewhat positive and somewhat negative) reply, and five is a definite yes. Have your special friend take the quiz, too, with you in mind. Then compare your answers. In this way, you can decide whether or not the intimate relationship you would like to have still has a long way to go.

The Intimacy Quiz

The *social aspect* of close companionship involves your behavior with each other in public. Do you:

_____ Know the other person's friends well?
_____ Have rapport with these friends?
_____ Encourage each other to meet new people and spend time with friends?
_____ Have a good rapport with the other's family and relatives?
_____ Enjoy participating in the same types of activities?
_____ Reach out or minister together to other people?

The *emotional area* concerns interaction on the level of a person's feelings. How well do the two of you communicate regarding the following:

_____ Concerns that affect you deeply?
_____ Feelings about your parents or others close to you?
_____ Habits of the other person that upset you?
_____ Experiences that have been joyful or painful?
_____ Negative reactions to other people or circumstances?
_____ Differences in your personalities?

The *mental aspect* deals with your thoughts and attitudes. How well do you know the other person in the area of:

_____ Honesty and integrity?

_____ The process he or she uses to make difficult decisions?

_____ Adjusting and compromising in a close relationship?

_____ Attitudes about children and family life?

_____ A sense of humor?

_____ Opinions about politics, national issues and current events?

_____ Ways of handling conflict and disagreements?

The *physical area* includes sexual factors, as well as those regarding personal physical well-being. Do each of you know:

_____ What physical qualities are attractive to the other person?

_____ What physical qualities are unattractive to the other?

_____ What sexual boundaries the other person respects?

_____ How the other controls his or her passions?

_____ The importance the other person places on various areas of personal physical fitness?

_____ How much effort the other is willing to give to keep up his or her standards of physical well-being?

The *spiritual aspect* deals with your religious or spiritual values and convictions. Do you know how strongly the following values or convictions affect the other person's daily living?

_____ Personal faith in God.

_____ Reliance upon the Bible for guidance.

_____ Belief in the death and resurrection of Christ.

_____ Importance of prayer.

_____ Biblical standards of morality.

_____ Hope of eternal life.

These five aspects of a person's life are interrelated and affect each other. None of them is isolated or unimportant.

As you progress in your knowledge of and experience with your companion, you will recognize the necessity for a mutual foundation and set of guidelines for developing harmony and intimacy in your relationship.

Qualities of Intimacy

The Bible gives eternal principles of living to help relationships be successful and fulfilling. Qualities that promote intimacy are discussed in Philippians 2:1-2. These can be applied specifically to a friendship and/or dating relationship. As you study these qualities of intimacy in Philippians, analyze your close relationships. How do they compare with this biblical pattern?

If some key areas have not been developed and show little hope for doing so, you may need to reconsider how dependent and intimate you should become with this person. On the other hand, if there is hope to build the relationship into this biblical pattern, you may be motivated to discuss the weaknesses of your association with the other person and develop a plan to strengthen that relationship.

> If therefore there is any encouragement in Christ,
> if there is any consolation of love,
> if there is any fellowship of the Spirit,
> if any affection and compassion,
> make my joy complete by being of the same mind,
> maintaining the same love,
> united in spirit,
> intent on one purpose (Philippians 2:1-2).

1. Encouragement in Christ

True intimacy starts with oneness with Christ. A relationship with the risen Savior brings His love, power and wisdom into your life. Only Christ can bring a change of heart and a strength to live His principles each day. The words *in Christ*, occur 133 times in the books written by the apostle Paul. To understand the importance of this term is to unlock the mysteries of a relationship. The word *in* means "within the sphere of." Like throwing an empty bottle into the ocean, it is soon surrounded and filled by — within the sphere of — the entire ocean.

In the same way, a person can be filled and surrounded by Christ in all His greatness. This relationship with Him is established by relying totally on the Lord for salvation and daily living. Without Him, we have only our frail human resources to achieve happiness, satisfaction and fulfillment.

Encouragement means to inspire with courage. As one of you faces difficulties, the other will offer a spirit of hope. You face challenges together so that, when one is weak, the other can be strong in Christ's strength. If both you and your friend have a commitment to Christ and a deep desire to obey Him in everything, you will be able to inspire one another in life's toughest spots.

2. Consolation of Love

When failure, pain, tragedy or disappointment strikes, comfort with tenderness is needed from the other. Consolation tries to alleviate grief or sense of loss.

When there are difficult times, the consolation of love desires to empathize and build up the other person. Consolation does not always involve looking for an answer. There are many times when there is no immediate or obvious answer for a situation. Many times consolation involves just listening as another pours out his or her thoughts and feelings.

For instance, a friend of mine broke his back a short while ago. The woman he dates did more than stick by him. She could not heal the break, but she did encourage him to handle the pain and to look for positive aspects in the middle of this tragedy. She helped him to entrust his life and future into the comforting arms of the Savior.

3. Fellowship of the Spirit

Contrary to the opinions of some people, Christian fellowship is not merely drinking coffee together and talking about the weather or the latest sports events. It means sharing a communion of hearts that have been brought together by the Holy Spirit. When we become Christians, the Holy Spirit within us gives us power to

live a fulfilling life and gives us oneness — fellowship of the
Spirit — with one another.

This is one reason why the Bible cautions against a heart
commitment to an unbeliever. When you try to be one with someone
who looks at life through eyes that do not include the eyes of the
Spirit, you can't become one with them without turning away from
the Holy Spirit.

As the apostle Paul said in 2 Corinthians 6:14,15, "Do not
be bound together with unbelievers; for what partnership have
righteousness and lawlessness, or what fellowship has light with
darkness? Or what harmony has Christ with Belial [a false god],
or what has a believer in common with an unbeliever?"

These verses apply to all close relationships that involve
dependency upon others. Even if one party is a Christian whose
life is committed more to self, to things or to anything other than
the Lord, this uneven relationship will negatively affect the walk
of faith of the more spiritual partner.

4. Affection and Compassion

Together, affection and compassion demonstrate tenderness
toward another person. Affection is a bond of caring and closeness
that does not involve romantic feelings. Compassion is mercy
extending itself to sympathize with another person's concerns.
Compassion wants to alleviate distress. Affection and compassion
see problems and reach out to try to solve them.

Christ got out of a boat and turned to see the masses of
people flocking after Him. "And disembarking, He saw a great
multitude, and He felt compassion for them because they were
like sheep without a shepherd, and He began to teach them many
things" (Mark 6:34). Matthew's account of the same incident states
that Jesus "felt compassion for them, and healed their sick"
(Matthew 14:14).

When the Lord saw needs, He was motivated by affection
and compassion to take the necessary steps to remedy the problems.
If we have experienced the ultimate solution for our own needs
by relying upon the Good Shepherd, we can show affection and
compassion to others.

5. Same Mind

To be like-minded doesn't mean that two people think the same thoughts. Being of the same mind means there is harmony in the midst of differences. It is important to express opinions and to speak your mind honestly. How you handle differences shows whether or not you are likeminded. If you are constantly arguing and bickering, you are not experiencing unity. Your deep desire for mental and emotional oneness is being frustrated.

Two people of like mind can interact from bases of unique individuality. Yet, when all has been said, they are at peace together.

6. Maintaining the Same Love

Falling in love takes little effort. The emotions seem to flow like a waterfall. But maintaining love takes work and commitment. It is easy to love when an atmosphere of romance envelopes you. But when things are going wrong and romantic feelings are at zero or below, it takes effort to keep love healthy.

When Paula and I bought our home in Dallas, the lawn looked beautiful and green. I mowed and watered it regularly. But, once I started my speaking schedule, we were out of town a lot. The lawn was neglected. Soon weeds and crab grass popped up through the beautiful lawn. Then ugly brown spots appeared and even uglier bugs infested the grass. A good lawn in Dallas demands constant attention and action. It has taken lots of effort, time and sweat to bring our lawn back to life again. How much easier it would have been had we been able to give it regular attention all along.

Maintenance is the life blood of love. So many forces can pull people apart and cause love to become weak and die. In *Beating the Break-Up Habit*, I explain the five major causes for the decline of a relationship and how to overcome them: communication gaps, unrealistic expectations, low self-image, selfishness and sexual burnout. To prevent these from destroying love, both persons must be committed to developing, to strengthening and to increasing their love. If they are not, a break-up is inevitable.

7. United in Spirit

The word *spirit* refers to the deep-down-inside you. To be united in spirit is to experience the union of your beings. You are woven together in your affection and in your souls. You determine that nothing will separate you.

To be united in spirit in a romantic relationship involves feelings but there is infinitely more. You are in touch with each other's inner character. No pretenses or facades exist. No dating games are played. Soul with soul form a single unit. Separate individuals are brought together by God and become "united in spirit." Then, when this results in marriage, they are made into "one flesh."

8. Intent on One Purpose

Two people in an intimate association come from different backgrounds, and different paths of life with different strengths and weaknesses, different experiences, different parents. But slowly their paths merge into one. Each continues to possess his or her own uniquenesses, but they find a harmony of direction toward the same goals in life.

Purpose in life includes much more than occupation, possessions, status, family and friendships. It involves a basic motivation for being alive and on this earth. The apostle Paul encourages the Christians of Rome to have the same purpose. "Now may the God who gives perseverance and encouragement grant you to be of the same mind with one another according to Christ Jesus; that with one accord you may with one voice glorify the God and Father of our Lord Jesus Christ" (Romans 15:5, 6).

Is it the deep desire of each of you to say, "Together, we want our lives and thoughts to reflect to the world our dependence on God?" If only one has this motivation, there will be discord no matter how much you love each other. This is a basic issue of life to settle.

A Catalyst for Harmony

A catalyst is a substance that causes two or more chemicals to react together. The list of qualities of intimacy in Philippians seem to be wonderful goals, but they are difficult to achieve. The catalyst that puts these qualities into action is given in verses three and four of Philippians 2. It is the attitude of humility.

Do nothing from selfishness or empty conceit, but with humility of mind let each of you regard one another as more important than himself. Do not merely look out for your own personal interests, but also for the interests of others (Philippians 2:3,4).

This attitude of humility cements a friendship. With it, there is no arrogance or malice. Without it, you try to construct a relationship where you can be in control. When a person constantly thinks of what he or she is getting from a relationship, that person is acting selfish and self- centered. It becomes hard to relax, to let go and to enjoy the other person. Such control can last only a short while.

Some people demand "their rights," which produces hurt feelings and barriers. Self-centered pride causes problems when it tries to manipulate the other person for selfish gain. You cannot control another person and have a sense of wholeness about self or about the relationship.

Instead of considering what is best for ourselves, we are to regard others as more important than ourselves. This may be hard to do, but it is rewarding. In *Make Love Your Aim*, Eugenia Price states it this way:

We show love, true love, when we concern ourselves first and always with the way the other person feels, not with how that other person is making us feel. . . . Our idea of love, based on over-sentimentality and romance, binds. Real love frees both parties to love more and still more and still more. As long as we are expecting, even demanding, that someone conform to our idea of love, we clamp chains on the loved one's heart. When we begin, however slowly, to free the loved one by acting ourselves on love as it is shown to us in the heart of God, we set the loved one free to begin to love us more.[2]

Christ is the ultimate example of humility. In Philippians 2:5-11, the verses immediately following Paul's explanation of humility, Paul explains Christ's sacrificial attitudes and actions toward us. He includes the statement:

Although He existed in the form of God, (He) did not regard equality with God a thing to be grasped, but emptied Himself, taking the form of a bondservant, and being made in the likeness of men. And being found in appearance as a man, He humbled Himself by becoming obedient to the point of death, even death on a cross (Philippians 2:6,7).

That is humility and compassionate love. Because Christ gave first toward us, we respond by giving back. That is the way humility works.

Now, to be humble doesn't mean you become a doormat for someone to walk all over your feelings and to use you. Christ humbled Himself to lay down His life for us, yet He was strong enough to stand for truth and righteousness. People did not run His life.

The building of an intimate association under Christ's influence develops these qualities of intimacy. As He draws two people together, they can build oneness and balance in the five areas of life. And, along the way, the exploring, developing, growing and discovering of one another is a challenge filled with adventure.

A Lopsided Star

When a greater importance is placed on one or two aspects of our five-pointed star of life, a relationship becomes unbalanced.

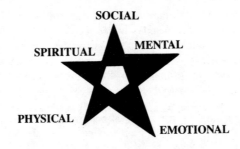

Physical Overemphasis

Overemphasis in the physical area usually results in a couple becoming involved in premarital intercourse or sharing sexual intimacies of foreplay. Such physical pressure affects the other areas negatively. In the emotional area, there is guilt, fear, anger or rejection. In the spiritual area, one grows cold toward God.

You don't want to be around Christians who seem to be happy or on fire for God if you are guilt-ridden about your activities. It is difficult to pray about your relationship. Because you feel guilt, you may be afraid that God will take the person away from you.

In the mental area, thinking about the other person is always focused on the physical. You plan the date hoping to end up making out. Because you don't yet know the person well in the other areas of his or her life, gnawing questions arise: "Does my lover love me just for my looks? For my body? For sex? How can my lover really love me for who I am? He (she) doesn't really know who I am!"

I remember seeing the beautiful movie star, Bo Derek, the original "10," being interviewed on television. As the third beautiful wife of John Derek, she was asked, "If you woke up tomorrow and found yourself disfigured by some disease, would your husband still love you?" Her answer? "I'm not sure." What a painful situation to be in, not knowing if the other person will accept you no matter what.

Social Overemphasis

Overemphasis on the social area of a relationship usually means that a couple may be putting on a happy face in public but cannot get along in private. Their friends may tell them, "You look so good and so right together." This becomes a subtle pressure to stay together even though they can't get along and are still undeveloped in other areas of their relationship.

Social overemphasis affects the emotions. If there is not a growing harmony, jealousy can erupt. One or both feel insecure in private. When one is talking or even looking at someone else, the other is jealous and angry.

Overemphasis on the social often drives them to become physically involved when they are in private for they have little else to enjoy when thye are alone together. If one of them has convictions about too much physical involvement, he or she may try to arrange for them to be alone together as little as possible.

Joyce and Dan are an example. They were a handsome couple, particularly on the tennis courts. Besides tennis, they enjoyed going to the movies, to parties and to church together. In none of these

activities did they have to relate intimately one on one, which was
fine with Dan. Unfortunately, Joyce had habits that irked Dan.
Other than their public activities, he felt they really had few
subjects of interest in common.

Joyce was a wonderful date but not Dan's kind of wife-material.
He felt he could keep dating Joyce for years but he didn't want
to marry her. After all, they did have fun in a crowd. And during
the little time they spent by themselves, Joyce was physically
affectionate. Other than romantic teasings, however, they said little
of substance to one another in private. But, on this basis, dating
Joyce was fun. It was also easier to keep dating Joyce than to
break it off and try to find someone else.

Finally, Dan saw that Joyce was expecting that something
more permanent might work out in the future. He knew then that
he had to stop the relationship. They broke up, but there was
bitterness on both sides. Dan and Joyce had fooled themselves to
accept fun and adventure and to neglect the more important qualities
of intimacy needed to build a relationship.

Spiritual Overemphasis

There can be overemphasis on the spiritual aspect of a relationship, too. There is an old saying, "You can become so heavenly
minded that you're no earthly good." A couple may emphasize
seeking the Lord's guidance and Bible reading to the exclusion of
common interests in their personalities and activities. When disagreements arise, they blame them on Satan rather than recognizing
that they have natural expectations and desires that conflict. Their
differences should be weighed when considering whether or not
God has intended them for one another.

The attitude of spiritualizing everything when considering a
potential mate causes some Christians to end up with less harmonious marriages than do non-Christians. An excellent marriage is
made up of two people who are good friends and good lovers. It
is built on friendship plus a Christ- centered oneness. Making God
the center of your relationship is essential, but don't spiritualize
everything to the neglect of recognizing and weighing your own
important differences.

Mental Overemphasis

And what might mental overemphasis be? Well, it's fun to talk about all kinds of subjects. When you first begin to date, you realize that there is a curiosity to know all you can about the other person. This is healthy and good. But don't use this curiosity to overlook the other dimensions of a relationship.

After one of my talks on dating and marriage, a man followed me out of the auditorium. "Excuse me," he said, "I need to get some advice about my girl friend. We have a lot of common interests and can talk about different subjects for hours. We have a great time together. We are headed toward marriage. But my main problem is that I'm not physically attracted to her. She doesn't excite me. We are good friends, but not potential lovers. Should we get married?"

I couldn't give him a definite yes or no. But I did caution him. "If you marry someone who is supposed to be the right one but you have little desire to be romantic and share physical love, then your marriage could be headed for catastrophe."

Emotional Overemphasis

An overemphasis on emotions often involves feelings of romance so overwhelming that one is blinded to any problems or potential problems in other areas. Often, a Christian will mistake exhilarating emotions for the leading of the Spirit. But is your natural spirit or the Holy Spirit leading you? When you allow your emotions to rule your head and your walk with God, basic differences can be considered unimportant. Insignificant areas of agreement may seem like important "signs from the Lord" on the rightness of your relationship.

You can become so enthralled with a person that you become unwilling to deal with any nagging doubts. If you cover over inner uneasiness and turmoil, it may result in psychosomatic illnesses such as ulcers or chest pains.

Jeannine, a Christian worker, was twenty-seven when she met Lawrence, a law student, at a Christian meeting. Soon Lawrence was paying a great deal of attention to her and helping with the meetings himself. Like others in the group, he began witnessing of Christ even to strangers.

Handsome, with an attractive personality, he soon had Jeannine in love, head over heels. In just a couple of months they announced their engagement. Everyone was very happy for them. They were an attractive couple who looked as if they would accomplish great things together for God.

However, one person was not sure about the relationship. Jeannine's roommate thought the romance had been too fast, too furious and too physically involved. When Jeannine was around Lawrence, she seemed to lose her emotional balance entirely. And why, her roommate wondered, was no one sure if Lawrence was a long-time Christian or a new one? But everyone else was so positive toward him that she felt her questions would seem petty and even smack of jealousy.

On the day of the wedding, the congregation waited and waited for the ceremony to begin. Finally, the minister came to the front and said that the bride had collapsed and had to be taken to the hospital. Everyone thought that it was merely nerves, pre-wedding jitters. The following day, Lawrence got the hospital chaplain to perform the wedding ceremony in the hospital room. The next day, against the wishes of her doctor, Lawrence signed Jeannine out of the hospital and they left for the Midwest, for their honeymoon and a new home.

Once he was back in law school, Lawrence soon found his studies kept him too busy for Christian friends. Soon he insisted that they start attending another church nearer their new home, one that was more socially prominent. He insisted on their spending all their social time with his old drinking buddies. He wanted Jeannine, who had never been around people who drank, to take an active part in their raucous times. When Jeannine tried to read her Bible, he became sullen and eventually angry. Nine months later, Jeannine, on the verge of a nervous breakdown, left her husband and returned to her parents' home.

Lawrence was possessed with a desire to become a politician. He certainly had the ability to get people to like him. When he first became involved with Jeannine's Christian group, he thoroughly enjoyed being around such up-beat people and wanted to be accepted as one of them. As always, he had no trouble adopting the enthusiasm and language of a new group. His attraction to Jeannine made him want to be a part even more. She met his criteria for a wife. He felt that, as a former Christian worker, and a beauty at that, she would make a good vote-getter in his home state in the Bible belt.

After the wedding, he focused back onto his original goal of politics. He felt he needed the support of his old friends in law school to help him on the road to a successful legal and political career. When Lawrence found that his efforts to manipulate Jeannine into the potential political wife he wanted had failed, he became interested in other women. Eventually, a divorce followed.

Jeannine had let her emotions and physical desires drown out the lack of mental and spiritual peace that she had had about Lawrence. Instead, it manifested itself in stomach pains and an attack of nerves on her wedding day. Even then, she refused to recognize her underlying uneasiness. Her roommate could have told her what was happening. But looking back on the situation, Jeannine admitted that, at the time, she was so captivated by Lawrence that she would not have listened to anyone.

Like many singles who have not had someone of the other sex in their lives for a long time, Jeannine was in love with love. One can enjoy the euphoria of emotions but refuse to accept wise counsel from friends or to admit to God that a person may not be "the right one." Breaking off this kind of a relationship means loneliness again and the embarrassment of admitting to friends and relatives that a wrong relationship had gone too far.

A lopsided star doesn't look right. In the same way, a lopsided relationship is unbalanced and will falter when it becomes necessary to put pressure on one of its undeveloped areas. The weak areas will create stress and disunity in the relationship.

Total life sharing means getting your star in shape. To last a lifetime, a relationship needs to develop harmony, knowledge and oneness in all aspects of life.

Even if you aren't dating anyone seriously at present, learn to develop the ingredients of a balanced friendship in your associations with the same or the other sex and with a relative or childhood friend. It's good to have strong, healthy friendships for several reasons:

(1) in order to understand and develop an ability for intimacy in dating and eventually in marriage;
(2) to give a broadened and balanced aspect to married life; and
(3) to give satisfaction in single life.

The prospect of marriage is put in a much more balanced view when you have intimate friendships. Then marriage is not looked to as the only answer to loneliness and to sharing yourself with someone else.

The next five chapters discuss each of these areas of life and relationships at length and give practical suggestions for strengthening intimacy and togetherness. As you read them, plan now as to how you can put a balanced star into your relationships.

---

1. In which areas of your relationships do you tend to be lopsided?

2. What role does humility play in your relationships?

3. How would you go about developing the qualities of intimacy contained in Philippians 2:1-2?

Chapter Eight
Relate in Public

THE
SOCIAL

It's becoming more and more common these days to have dimmers on light switches. You can turn the lights on low, then slowly turn the dimmer switch and watch the lights get brighter and brighter. No matter where you are in your relationship with the other sex, at any point from pitch blackness to the brilliance of sunlight, perhaps I can help you turn up the dimmer button to become a better friend and a better lover.

The French saying, vive la difference — long live the difference — says it beautifully. Men and women are very different people. However, I want to stress that men and women are not complete opposites. They have more aspects in common than they have that are different. So while I stress their differences in this chapter, instead of using the popular term, the opposite sex, I prefer to use the term, the other sex.

One of the clearest indications I've had of a genuine, deep difference between men and women occurred when I was the director for the Campus Crusade for Christ ministry at the University of Georgia, where I had three women on my staff. As I was growing up, I had two brothers, but no sisters. So relating to women just as people was a bit of a mystery to me.

One day, traveling back to my home in Athens, Georgia, I saw some beautiful wild flowers, actually flowering weeds, along the roadside. I stopped and picked some. After getting back in town I wondered what to do with them. I didn't own a vase so I decided to take them to the staff women's apartment.

When I knocked on their door, Becky opened it. Offhandedly, I explained that I had seen some wild flowers alongside the road and had picked them. When I asked Becky if she would like them, I was met with immediate exuberance. "Flowers? Real flowers? For us?" Taken aback, I stammered, "They're only weeds." Ignoring my reply, she shouted to her two roommates who came running. "Look, everyone, Dick just brought us flowers!"

No one could have been more welcome to those women that day than I with that handful of flowering weeds. I got the royal treatment. When I left their apartment, I had absolutely no doubt that women look at life differently, particularly when it comes to simple things.

Living Life to the Fullest

My reason for presenting differences in looking at the institution of dating is not to give all the latest ideas about how to get married. I present these differences in order to show how to *understand* and *enjoy* the other sex, so that you can develop the social aspect of intimacy with them and live life to the fullest socially while still a single individual.

I was single for forty-two years of my life and always wanted to get married. There were times when I thought I never would. There were also times, while dating certain women, that I hoped I wouldn't!

As a single, I saw that many single people waste their lives waiting for the right person to come along. Then, and only then, do they think they'll start enjoying life. I believe in living life to the fullest where you are right now. There is never a place in the Bible where it says that marriage makes you happy. It says over and over again that God makes you happy.

Now, obviously, we have to relate to one another, enjoy each other and function as members of the body of Christ, If what I share about being a friend and a lover leads to marriage, fine. If it doesn't, fine. I want to help you experience to the greatest degree all that God has for you right now and to encourage you to let Him take care of the future.

Right Attitudes Spawn Right Relationships

No matter what your situation, attitudes toward the other sex are important. You may be attracted to them in general or just to some individuals whom you think are very special. On the other hand, members of the other sex may puzzle you. You may be attracted to them but you can't figure them out. Just when you think you finally understand them, they do something that totally puzzles you.

You may be intimidated by the other sex. In the past, you may have had difficult times with them and struggled in the area of relationships. You may feel distrustful of the other sex. You may have been hurt in the past, whether in dating relationships or in family relationships as a child. You may have had great expectations and dreams; promises may have been made and then broken. Maybe you exposed your heart and then found it betrayed. Whatever your pleasure or pain in past relationships, you can grow. There is hope for developing intimacy in the social area of your people-relating star.

Through the years, I felt very confident in many areas, including my chosen profession. But in relationships with women I felt very intimidated. Many times, I would like some woman very much but just would not know how to communicate with her. I could talk to everyone else except the one I wanted to talk to most. Through all my dating and relating, I have learned some principles that have become like windows to understanding the other sex.

Treat a Woman Like a Woman

I personally believe that one of the greatest desires of a woman's heart is to be special. I notice that women use that word *special* a lot, but men don't seem to do so. A woman will often

say that a man is special to her or that she wants to be special
to someone. Even on a first date with an attractive man, a woman
may hope that she sparks in him a special interest.

Women want to feel that the man interested in them cares.
The saying, "little things mean a lot," opens the door to a woman's
heart. This presents a problem to many men who go along in life
oblivious to little kindnesses and courtesies.

I was at a large conference in Philadelphia where my friend
and former college roommate, Josh McDowell, was to speak.
Close to midnight the night before his scheduled men's seminar
on sex and dating, he called me into his room and said, "Dick,
I'm really sick. I don't think I can speak tomorrow morning. Why
don't you take my place?"

"But what'll I say?" was my immediate response as I began
to panic.

I called my girl friend and said, "I'll be speaking to five
hundred men tomorrow morning about women. If you had that
opportunity, what would you say to them?"

Without hesitation, she said, "I would tell them to treat a
woman like a woman."

I wasn't sure I had understood her, so later in our conversation
I said, "Tell me again, what would you tell these men?"

She repeated the same words, "Treat a woman like a woman."
After we hung up, I wondered what she meant. How do you treat
a woman like a woman? I stayed up much of the night trying to
incorporate her ideas into my speech.

Several months later I conducted a seminar on "Becoming a
Friend and Lover" at a large church in Houston. One participant
asked me, "How do you feel about men who treat a woman like
a buddy? The non-Christian men at work treat me like a lady but
Christian men treat me like a buddy. I don't want to pursue a
relationship with any of the non-Christians because they want sex
by the third date. But the Christian men I know aren't interested
in dating so what do I do?"

By the end of this book, I hope I will have answered that
question. But right here I urge the men to open their eyes. Women
don't want to be treated like a buddy. Even if a man isn't personally
interested in the women in his circle of acquaintances, he ought
to treat them differently than he would a buddy. Don't take a

woman for granted. For instance, if a woman you work with does a good job, why not tell her? Let her know that she is special enough to warrant a compliment.

How To Ask for a Date

Now, if you are interested in asking a woman for a date, remember that she wants to feel special. Don't say, "Hi, what are you doing Friday night?" Now, I know a man asks that way because he doesn't want to hear a, "No, I have other plans." He likes to cover all his bases first. He can be pretty sneaky in doing this. He tries to find out from her or her friends what her plans are for that weekend. After knowing this, then he asks the casual question, "What are you doing Friday night?"

The problem is that this leaves the woman in a very insecure position. It's hard for her to know how to respond to that question. If she likes the man, she doesn't want to come on like a tiger and say, "I'm not doing anything that I wouldn't drop in order to go out with you! What do you have in mind?" After all, she thinks, what if he should say, "Oh, nothing," and then just walk away!

On the other hand, if she doesn't like the man, she has a dilemma. If she says she's busy that night, what if a close friend of his, whom she does like, asks her out for the same night? She won't want to say to him, "I have plans."

First impressions are important. A man needs to consider what he thinks a woman might like to do on a date. Then he should ask her a definite question. "Hey, there's a great concert coming up Friday night. Would you like to go to dinner and the concert with me?" She can then give a definite reply without revealing whether or not she's more interested in going out with him or in going to the concert. There's time to decide that later.

Even if a man starts a relationship by asking for specific dates, later on it's easy for him to slide into a rut in date planning. After awhile, too many guys just say, "Well, what do you want to do Friday night?"

Then the woman will reply, "I don't know, what would you like to do?"

And the guy will come back with, "I don't know. What do you think?" Many women have told me how exasperated they become with a man's indecisiveness.

By the time a man has been dating a woman awhile, he should have all kinds of ideas of what she likes and doesn't like to do. But he has to be sensitive if he is going to find out these things. She's not likely to tell them to him directly. She wants him to learn to understand her desires without her saying, "This is what I like." Such little things mean a lot to a woman.

For instance, when my wife Paula was pregnant, she needed to walk every day. So, whenever she was ready, I would drop what I was doing and walk with her. After the baby was born, she told me, "Dick, I know that you truly love me."

"Really?" I said. "How do you know that?"

"Because you walked with me every day, when I knew you didn't always want to do it."

It's the little things that say, "I love you."

Men and the Respect Syndrome

On the other hand, a man usually wants to be respected. Obviously, men want to be special, too, and women want to be respected. But it's strange to a woman that a man wants to be respected above all else. To a man, it seems that if he can get respect, then a woman will love him. Of course, this philosophy rarely works well, since a man often works hard at a job, at sports or some other activity trying to gain respect, and ends up losing his wife or girl friend because he didn't pay enough attention to her. Men have a hard time learning that respect doesn't automatically carry over into love. The way to the top may not be the path to her heart.

For instance, when I started to become a traveling speaker, I was dating a woman back home in Indiana. One day she told me that she didn't want to date me any more. I was astounded. I said, "Come on, you really want to break up with me?" Although I didn't say it out loud, what I was thinking was, *Do you really know who you are dating?*

She wasn't impressed with my position. What she wanted was caring commitment and I hadn't given her that.

Men have this funny attitude. "Well, look at my job, look at how I do in sports. You should love me because I'm respected by others." A man hasn't learned that receiving respect doesn't tie into love. As a responder, a woman is more likely to love you when you show her love first, instead of a reason for her to respect you.

The Bible says that a man should love his wife. To love your wife means to show her that she is special. The Bible also says that a woman should be subject to her husband. A woman may love a man but will she want to be responsive to his leading? She will be responsive if she respects and admires him, first of all for what he is, only secondarily (and maybe not at all) for what he does. For a woman, love leads into respect, rarely the other way around.

Now, how can a woman begin to build respect for a man and then show him this respect? One way is to discover a man's strengths and to encourage him to develop those strengths. Another way is to show him that you really believe in him. A man often gets discouraged (as do women) and it always helps to have someone say, "I respect you, I believe in you, and I want to encourage you."

How To Refuse a Date

Even if a woman isn't interested in dating a certain man, she can show that she still respects him in the way that she turns him down. Of course, a lot of women are wondering how they can get a date, not turn one down. Nevertheless, let's look at the possibility of being in a position of being able to turn down a date.

I've had girls turn me down for a date in such a way that I vowed to God I would never ask them for anything again, not even for the time of day. A woman can obliterate a man by the way she turns him down for a date. That's one reason some men don't date.

Now women may think this is just that old male ego getting stepped on and believe that men put too much stock in it. Some women even rationalize that it probably does men good to suffer a little rejection. But just remember, women have egos too. The difference is that the man usually takes the outward initiative in dating, even if the woman has been working on it subtly for months. Before he asks her out, he may assume she likes him enough to go out with him, but her little hints haven't told him that for sure. So, when he makes that first outward initiative, he has to lay his emotions on the line by revealing definitely that he likes her enough to want to go out with her.

In her reply, however, a woman doesn't have to reveal her feelings whatsoever. "I'm so sorry. I'm going out of town this weekend," could mean any of the following:

"I wish I weren't going out of town and could go out with you."

"Maybe I would be interested in going out with you sometime."

"I need some time to think about it."

"I'm sure glad I have an excuse not to go out with you!"

"I hate to lie about going out of town, but I would do anything to get out of going on a date with you!!"

And you still wonder why a man often becomes timid in asking for dates?

When I was single, there were many, many weekends when I didn't have a date. Not because I had tried and couldn't get one. I was sensitive to the possibility of getting my feelings hurt by a negative reply.

So how should a woman handle a request for a date? If you don't want to go out, I think it's quite all right to say, the first time, that you're busy that night. You don't have to tell what your plans are and the man shouldn't ask. It's none of his business that you just may plan to watch television.

A woman wants a man to initiate a dating relationship, but she wants the right man to do so. The problem is, neither of them know if he is the right man. We've heard stories about men who kept asking, asking and asking a woman for months and even years, before she would finally go out. Then they ended up getting married. But, generally, if a guy is asking you out a lot and you don't want him to continue, you should be open, honest and straightforward. By the third invitation, simply say, "I appreciate your asking me, but I don't want to have a dating relationship with you."

That's tough to do, particularly since a woman would rather a man pick up on her subtle hints that she isn't interested. But a man's mind isn't tuned in to picking up subtle hints. He needs to hear it straight. He senses that you, at least, respect him if you tell him honestly.

A woman should always remember that a man wants to hear it straight. When I speak to an all-male audience, I lay my message on the line. The straighter and more accurate I am in getting to the point with a group of men, the better they love it. But I can't do that when I speak to an all-female audience. It comes across too harshly. I have to talk around a subject before I finally get to the point. Women are usually softer, more sensitive people.

The Band-Aid illustration shows the difference. When I was a little boy, I would try to take a Band-Aid off a cut. Now, there were two ways to take it off. One was my way. The other was my mother's way. My way was to pull it off slowly, hair by hair, so that it wouldn't hurt. Of course, it still hurt for the hour it would take me to get it off that way. My mother would come over and see me trying to take off the Band-Aid, and say, "Oh, you want to take it off? Here, I'll help you." In the flick of an eye, she had it ripped off while I was left howling at the top of my lungs. There was pain either way, but at least with my mother's quick and easy method, I got over the pain faster.

The point is that it is easier for a man and woman to end the uncertainty of parrying over going out if the woman will simply tell her feelings straight out and get it over with. Then, if he keeps asking her, she has freedom to say, "I've already told you. I would like to be your friend but I don't want to have a dating relationship." It may hurt him, but he will appreciate your openness and show of respect for him. If you try to tell him only through subtle hints, he is likely to take a very long time to get the message. When he does, he probably will blame you for stringing him along for so long, even though your intention was just the opposite.

Love and Good Deeds

For those who have begun a dating relationship, Hebrews 10:23-25 tells us that we are to stimulate one another to love and good deeds. In the social area, we need to pray fervently that the Lord will give us wisdom, that we would respect each other, that we would consider each other special. For a man, this means doing the small things for a woman like holding a door. For a woman, it means helping a man think through a problem that he is facing and giving him encouragement.

Of course, sometimes you can get your signals mixed. While I was in Illinois on a speaking tour, I had a couple of dates with a woman who wanted to do everything for herself. She promptly let me know she would rather open her own doors and seat herself in restaurants. Shortly thereafter, I went home to Texas where I had several dates with a girl I had known awhile. At the end of the fourth date, she told me, "I want to talk with you ."

"Oh, what about?" I replied.

"You never open a door for me. You never pull out my chair. You never help me out of the car!"

I was shell-shocked. What different expectations these two women had. There will be exceptions and we will have to learn how to flex and treat each other as individuals.

Special Thoughts for Special Dating

Dating is much more than looking for a potential mate or having a good time. It is the beautiful opportunity of influencing someone else's life and having yours influenced, too. Make it a godly, positive experience. Cultivate healthy attitudes that will enhance a friendship and give depth to your caring. The following are some special thoughts you might remember in this regard.

1. Play the field until you get up to bat.

People are fascinating. The variety of people's personalities, interests, concerns and behavior is almost infinite. Get to know lots of different people rather than focusing on one type. The broader your exposure to different people, the clearer your picture of the kind of person you would like to settle down with.

Follow the example of my friend Tony who wasn't interested in getting serious with anyone. He decided to date lots of women just to be sociable and to have something to do on weekends. He didn't act too serious toward any woman but was friendly and interested in each one. Although Tony was average in looks, his friendliness attracted many women to him. I was curious as to how he kept eight women wanting to date him.

From Tony, I found out not to worry about what people may think of you. Down-to-earth friendliness and kindness are wonderful virtues. A negative reputation comes from making promises you don't keep or from being a superficial flirt.

If you date more than one person simultaneously, treat each one honestly and respectfully. Don't get involved romantically with any of them. As soon as you become involved, you are subtly committing yourself to that person. If you do that with a couple of people, you will get into trouble. Sooner or later, hidden activities come to the surface.

When you get tired of playing the field and want to get to first base with one person, show special interest and attention. Slowly or quickly (depending on your circumstances), stop dating others and then date the person you like exclusively. Don't keep playing the field, even in your mind. You can be attracted to many but truly love only one. Trouble comes when you grow in your commitment with one person while, at the same time, you keep others around for "social security." Don't develop a fickle heart. "Let love be without hypocrisy" (Romans 12:9).

2. Fun is having a good time without a guilt hangover.

"We had a great time!" That's what we want to be able to say about a date. Fun, excitement, laughs, satisfaction. The real test of a date, however, is not the response to the activities of one night or one day. It's the attitudes and mental, emotional and spiritual health that are produced through being together over a period of time.

The Bible is the Christian's guidebook for behavior. It gives principles of interacting with people and with circumstances that will lead us to personal and relational health. For instance, the Bible says "Abhor what is evil. Cling to what is good" (Romans 12:9).

Keep your heart and conscience under the control of the Holy Spirit. Let the Scriptures saturate your mind and your dating activities. If the person you date asks you to do questionable things, be strong and say no. It's much easier to say no to a person than to say "I'm sorry" to God.

It is real fun to enjoy being with someone who encourages you in your walk with God. With God at the center of your relationship and activities, you are free to love and be loved with a love greater than your own, the love that includes His strength and guidance.

3. Be a builder, not a demolitions expert.

As you get to know a person more closely, you begin to see flaws that you didn't notice in the beginning. In fact, it may be beyond your comprehension why anyone would do what your date just did! Some of his or her actions may not only upset you, they may infuriate you. Little annoyances can become major land mines.

What do you do in such a case? Too many people air their frustrations about the other in public with belittling and sarcastic remarks. One couple I know claimed to love one another, but by the way they talked about each other, I had my doubts. At parties and in other groups, they would air their differences, laughing sarcastically at each other's idiosyncrasies.

One night Paula and I double-dated with them. During that evening they expressed their sorrow about their behavior toward one another. They decided instead to build each other up and to show respect. I applauded their mature decision.

Dating is building the foundation of a long-term relationship. You may not end up marrying each other, but, in dating, you are developing either a long-term friend or potential adversary. Some of us hold grudges for years after a person has put us down.

It is better to build good memories each time you get together. Then, in the future, you can look back on them with a smile. The apostle Paul said, "Be devoted to one another in brotherly love; give preference to one another in honor; not lagging behind in diligence, fervent in spirit, serving the Lord" (Romans 12:10,11).

4. Your public life reflects the quality of your private life.

A person is considered a phony when what he or she says doesn't match personal actions. I grew up hearing my father say, "What you do speaks louder than what you say." Talk is cheap.

Notice the amount of consistency between intimate conservations and public behavior. Is the other person (or are you) faithful to personal promises? Beware of (and don't become) the individual who says "I love you" in private but acts like the object of that love doesn't exist when around other people.

If you build integrity in your private life, it will show in your public life. We are told that we should be:

"Rejoicing in hope,
persevering in tribulation,
devoted to prayer,
contributing to the needs of the saints [all Christians],
practicing hospitality" (Romans 12:12,13).

The first three of these are private activities. Hope is founded on God's Word. Cling to Him in troubles and disappointments. Devote yourself to prayer and talking with God.

If you do, your life will exhibit the last two activities which are practiced in public. Out of a full heart, dedicated to God, you will help others in need. You will be generous and hospitable, opening your home and yourself to entertain and provide for others. You will treat others as you would like to be treated.

Do you and the person you date have these desires? It is important as a couple to be kind and giving to others. Why don't the two of you throw a party for friends and invite new people from outside your clique to come? Make them feel at home and welcome.

5. An honest, spontaneous compliment is a bouquet of thrills.

Have you ever tried to manipulate a compliment out of someone? You want them to notice your new hairstyle, your new car, your latest achievement or the good deed you've just done.

When they don't say anything, you're hurt. So you drop hints, hoping they will react with a favorable and vocal response. When they finally do, you're grateful. But it doesn't satisfy as much as if they had noticed spontaneously.

On the other hand, when someone gives you a completely unexpected compliment, you are thrilled. What a surprise! For the rest of the day you think about it.

Learn to notice the details. Be honest, with some elation, about what pleases you, but without being overbearing and gushy.

Too much of a good thing seems forced. Become a salt shaker of compliments, giving enough to be appreciated and to flavor your relationship. When you think something is nice, say so.

Also, learn to take a compliment. It always irked me when a girl would respond to my compliment with a negative statement.

"I like your hair."

"Oh, it needs cutting so badly."

"That's a pretty dress."

"Really? It's so old."

"Your dinner was delicious."

"Well, it didn't come out as well as I had planned, but I'm glad it was edible."

"You sing so well."

"Oh, I need to practice a lot more than I do."

When someone compliments you, simply say, "Thank you." Then say no more. When you tag your thanks with some remark that belittles the object of the compliment, you belittle the other person's taste or opinion. Many people do this in a false attempt to show personal humility rather than personal pride, but the effect backfires. The person giving the compliment ends up feeling humiliated. Just show gratefulness for kind words and leave it at that.

"Let your speech always be with grace, seasoned, as it were, with salt, so that you may know how you should respond to each person" (Colossians 4:6).

6. Friends are the window to a person's character.

If you want to know what is important in the life of the person you are dating, study that person's close friends. As they say, "Birds of a feather flock together." Friends often reflect a person's values, personality, habits, attitudes and opinions. Obviously, the friends will differ from the one you are dating in certain areas and even disagree completely on some things. But the reason they are close friends is that they share similar ideas and interests.

Do you enjoy the other person's friends? Can you get along together? If not, it may be a sign that, once married, when you both relax and stop putting your best foot forward, you may have the same problems in getting along with your mate as you did with his or her friends before the marriage.

If the person doesn't have friends, it may indicate that he or she has a difficult time developing relationships, or prefers to be a loner. If so, you must consider if this is the type of person you want to marry.

Parents usually know a person better than anyone. How does your dating partner treat them? Is there care, love and affection between them? Or are there tensions, arguments and misunderstandings? The way a person treats parents and relatives is a good indicator of how you eventually will be treated.

Now you may want to excuse your dating partner if the parents are divorced or just plain cantankerous. But, if this is so, it means that your dating partner may not have learned from them how to relate with other people while growing up. Learning to relate in the home is intended to be part of the growing-up process.

Your date may have learned what not to do in relating with other people, but has that person since learned and put into practice how to relate with other people? If not, when in a tough relational situation, he or she is likely to revert to reactions seen practiced during childhood.

7. *Keep the child in you alive.*

Children are curious about everything. Their minds delve into all kinds of areas that are mysteries to them. They are not afraid to ask questions and seek answers.

As a one-year-old, my daughter Rachel loved to play with ordinary household objects. When you lose the desire to find something new and exciting in ordinary things, you will become dull and boring. Too many people become so serious about daily existence and its problems that they forget to be thrilled and excited about the ordinary things of life.

Become an interesting person by developing an interest in life and in other people. Ask questions and listen intently to answers. Together enjoy the simple things in life — walking in the park, reading, watching an ant hill, going window shopping, looking at the stars, smelling flowers. Develop a sense of curiosity and enjoyment about God's world and life itself.

One of the best dates I ever had could have been a disaster. I had planned to take Chris to a nice restaurant and then to a movie. After the meal, the waitress brought the check and I gave her my credit card. "I'm sorry," she said, "we don't take credit cards here." So I whipped out my wallet, paid the bill in cash, and left a tip.

Then I counted what was left. $3.54. What do I do now? Panicking and almost unable to speak, I considered the situation. Finally I thought of an idea. I said, "Chris, tonight you have a great opportunity. We are going to do something special, a change of plans." I showed her my wallet. "I'm going to give you all my money, all of it, with two stipulations. First of all, you have to spend all of it, every penny. Second, you have to take me along."

I then proceeded, laboriously, to pull out three one-dollar bills and fifty-four cents in change, a coin at a time. The astonished look on her face made me even more uneasy, but I kept going with my idea. "Let's think of the good points of this situation. I didn't know this restaurant wouldn't take credit cards, but we can still have a great time, if we try, with $3.54."

So we sat there, trying to decide what to do. It was tough at first. Do you know how many things you can buy for $3.54?

As we started to go around town with our money, we went into a number of department stores that didn't seem to have anything interesting for $3.54. Finally, we ended up in a cheap discount store, looking at balloons. You can buy a lot of balloons for $3.54. But as we thought about sitting around all night trying to blow them up, we decided against that idea. Finally, we settled on a puzzle for $3.10 and a mutilated candy bar on a table of odds and ends for $.24. With tax, they added up to exactly $3.54. Making our purchases took two hours.

We then went to Chris's apartment, laughing about our unique treasure hunt. We made the mashed candy bar last the rest of the evening, and we worked on the puzzle. It was a great time, a date I'll always remember. So learn to be creative and enjoy the simple things.

Two Roads

Relating together socially is part of learning how to mold two distinct lives toward a common unit. Two roads begin to merge into one with all their twists and turns. Yet there will always be differences. That can be intriguing — as well as irritating.

You may decide that the differences in interests and behavior prohibit a serious relationship. It is a mature person who allows this realization to be the crossroad where each goes a separate way, but richer and wiser for the experience of their time together.

But if you decide you appreciate each other's social outlook and habits enough to work out the differences, then social intimacy can be a rich experience in building toward a successful marriage or just toward a beautiful friendship.

---

1. What are some of the differences you've found between the sexes?

2. What difficulties do you have in relating with persons of the other sex?

3. What are some of the areas that need to be strengthened in the social area in your relationships?

Chapter Nine
Have a Meeting of Your Minds

SOCIAL

THE MENTAL

No matter how much we appreciate people, we have to realize that those we love and respect most are still going to think different from the way we do in certain areas. While it's true that opposites attract, opposites also make sparks. No matter what kinds of relationships you have, they are going to involve big differences.

When Paula and I got married, we found our different ways of doing things clashed most at the grocery store. You see, Paula hates to shop, so she always maps out a plan of action, her P.O.A. She thinks through exactly what she wants to get beforehand, makes a list and then looks only for the items on that list.

Not me! I love shopping! I look forward to going to a grocery store and seeing the various shapes, sizes and colors of everything. What's more, when I go to a store, it's a vacation for me. I'm away from my desk and from the telephone. No one can reach me. I love to walk up and down each aisle, absorbing myself in everything that's there.

When we first started shopping together, I would saunter down the aisles taking in everything. Paula would zip, zip, zip from one section to another, grabbing only what she had already decided to buy. She would say, "Dick, come on, hurry up!" and I would say, "Honey, do you know that they have five different brands of yogurt and I like all five? I can't decide which brand I want to get or which flavors."

After awhile, we learned that when we shop together, we have to have a mutual P.O.A. Paula says, "Dick, you get the bread." That's the only responsibility I have. She gets twenty items and I get the bread. By the time she gets her twenty items, I'm still looking at the bread. I want to get bread with all the right ingredients and with no preservatives. And yet I want to get the best-tasting and the most economical bread as well. I may take a long time, but I leave the grocery store satisfied that I've made the very best choice of bread for us.

Now, we could have solved the problem differently. We could have agreed never to go to the grocery store together. But that might have carried over to not going many other places together. I could have insisted that she learn to saunter along with me, while she got more and more anxious about spending so much time aimlessly. Or, to keep peace, I might have rushed through the store with her, becoming frustrated that I had no opportunity to check out new items or to experience the sense of rejuvenation I get from losing myself in a grocery store.

Unique in Our Oneness

Those inadequate solutions, would have violated what, I be-lieve, is the primary goal in relating with someone of the other sex (or, for that matter, relating with anyone). That goal is to preserve that person's uniqueness. The other person is a unique creature of God who thinks differently. You need to learn to understand the other person as much as possible.

One in Our Uniqueness

The second goal in establishing a relationship is to build unity, preserving each person's uniqueness while building oneness in the relationship. Oneness doesn't mean thinking the same way. It's never good to force another person to think like you do, for as

in the old saying, "If two are the same, one is not needed."
Consider the apostles Peter and Paul. They thought very differently
but they had oneness of mind in serving the Lord.

In writing about oneness between men and women, the apostle
Peter said, "To sum up, let all be harmonious, sympathetic,
brotherly, kindhearted, and humble in spirit; not returning evil for
evil, or insult for insult, but giving a blessing instead; for you
were called for the very purpose that you might inherit a blessing"
(1 Peter 3:8, 9). This doesn't mean that each person in a relationship
should think exactly the same. You'll never find two people who
do that. "Let all be harmonious" means that you learn to build
oneness together. To be likeminded is to have the same goals and
purposes as you serve the Lord together.

God has given each of us different gifts. Sometimes it seems
that some of the gifts don't mesh. You'll have one person who is
outgoing, bubbly, active, hopping quickly from one exciting idea
and plan to another. Another person is slow about things and wants
to think deeply before making any move at all. This is usually
the one who sees all the little details and presents all the reasons
why an idea won't work. He or she tends to pour cold water on
the onslaught of ideas that the effervescent person is certain can
be carried out.

The cautious thinker gears down the other. If it weren't for
Mr. or Miss Cautious, Mr. or Miss Gung-Ho would head toward
their common goal in overdrive, outdistancing everyone else. Eventually, however, the Gung-Ho person either strips the energy gears
or crashes into a brick wall, because there's no control on momentum
when an obstacle appears in the path. At the same time, Mr. or
Miss Cautious wouldn't even get into first gear, if it weren't for
the enthusiastic ideas of Mr. or Miss Gung-Ho. Those God-given
traits that seem to clash were given to us for a purpose — to help
us balance one another.

God wants us to learn to work together in a coordinated
manner. This applies to all relationships in life. By appreciating
the God-given character traits of people who are different from
us, we can work together to accomplish God's purposes.

Instead of either Paula or I saying to the other, "You've got
to be like me," we have learned to preserve each other's uniqueness
while working on oneness, not only on shopping trips but in other
areas of our lives as well.

The Joy of Discovery

Across America, one of the questions I hear often is, "Why don't men communicate more?" I don't think it's because men can't talk. I think it's because men don't learn to keep talking about their own lives. They can talk for hours with a colleague about their work or with a fellow enthusiast about a favorite sport or hobby. Other than that, men talk in short sentences about themselves and their own feelings and opinions.

Women, on the other hand, love details. Have you ever noticed the difference between a man and a woman when answering a simple question? You ask a man, "Was Joe at the party last night?" "Yeah, he was there," is the only reply you'll get.

Ask a woman the same question and she is likely to reply, "Sure, Joe was there. I didn't like what he was wearing, though. His wild shirt and belt didn't match anything he had on. You know, I think he looks so awkward on the dance floor. Someone needs to give him dance lessons."

Most women are interested in details, feelings and opinions. They assume other people are too. We men need to learn to be more detail oriented. Talk details and a woman will love it.

To be of the same mind as someone else, which is an important part of developing intimacy, you must discover how another person thinks and allow the other person to learn how you think. Developing the mental area of our star of intimacy can be a fascinating journey. Let's consider some ideas on how to discover what is in someone else's mind.

1. Discover how the other person makes decisions.

Is he or she logical in approaching life? Does this person get all the facts together and then make a decision? Or does he make a decision quickly and then change that decision several times, going back and forth on what should be done? Does this person contemplate a situation a long time before making a decision, then, having made it, refuse to reconsider? Or does he decide, and then, holding to that decision, continually worry if it is right, which hinders carrying out the decision? Learning the decision process that other people use is important to understanding those people.

2. Learn how the other person listens.

Is he always talking and never listening? For instance, have you ever been in two conversations at once, actually two monologues that constitute a conversation? You say something. That reminds the other person of another subject so he interrupts you with his own statement. You pay no attention to what he is now saying because you're only waiting to continue what you were saying in the first place. This is not a meeting of the minds.

Some people must have an opportunity to complete their communication before they can switch mental gears toward listening to someone else. Learn how the other person listens. Then gear your conversations to each other's ways of listening.

3. Learn how to ask questions.

I have been amazed at the number of people who don't know how to question others. They communicate only in statements.

Whenever the other person makes a statement, don't let that be the end of the communication. For example, you may say, "How did your work go today?"

"Okay," the other person says.

And that's the end of the conversation. You have to find another subject to discuss but with such limited answers, you run out of subjects quickly.

Learn to question a person about a subject. A key to doing this is by using the little word *explain*. "Explain to me what you did today at work." Other helpful words include the journalist's basic newsgathering formula, the five "w"'s and "h" — *who, what, why, where, when,* and *how*. "Who did you talk with today at work?" "What is the most important project you've worked on this week?" "Why do you like (or dislike) your work?" "When do you hope to finish that big project you're working on?" "How do you accomplish this project?" If you use these key words, the person will have to talk more.

4. Discover the other person's opinions.

Ask questions that reveal the other person's opinions and how those opinions were formed. Why does the person think the way he does on such subjects as politics, sports, and war? As time goes on, especially in marriage, knowing why another person thinks in a particular way becomes more and more important.

5. Expand your conversations.

Communication can be fun. It shouldn't be seen as a dull way to pass the time. Expand your mind, read books and literature and learn to talk intelligently on subjects besides the weather and sports. Read a weekly news magazine and discuss something in it that interests you or the other person. Learn to discuss certain issues in life that are affecting people.

If you marry, you will spend thousands of hours alone with that person. If your time alone now is primarily a make-out scene, you will have a hard time in marriage finding something to do together for a lifetime. All evening long, five nights a week, plus the forty-eight hours that make up Saturday and Sunday, year in and year out, require something more than physical attraction to enjoy each other's company continually.

Although, at first, we are all attracted to another person's outward appearance, eventually that person's body deteriorates. The mind and character of the person, however, can keep on growing and growing. That should be the more important focus as we seek a mate.

Instead of communicating like two ships passing in the night, ask questions, listen, and then think through the other person's statements.

Sharing Your Minds

I like antiques and I like to teach other people about them. I think one of the greatest ways to have fun with someone else is to go to an antique auction. It doesn't cost a thing unless you raise your hand. Just watching the auctioneer is an experience in itself. Playing a guessing game about the sale price for an item is a great trivial pursuit. You try to learn why one item goes for five dollars and another for five hundred.

For years, I looked forward to the prospect of teaching and enjoying antiquing with my future mate. What a blow it was to learn that Paula didn't take to it the way I did. But she knows how much I enjoy looking at antiques so she learned to appreciate it more for my sake. At the same time, we have found that interests we never expected to share with someone are the ones we enjoy the most.

I'm sure that you must have a favorite interest that you can share with another person. In fact, you should have more than one, in case the other person isn't eager to learn about your very favorite interest. At the same time, be open to learning about the other person's interests, even if the subjects never attracted you before.

Differences Require Commitment

An important part of the mental area of relationships concerns how to handle differences. Working out differences is a major problem in today's fast-paced, changeable world. Today, most people go by the all-American rally cry, "Get in there and quit!" Sometimes I think our modern world is made up of nothing but quitters who, if they don't like something or find it difficult, just drop it and go on to something else. Commitment has become a foreign word in our society. When is the last time you heard someone say they were committed to anything, except to a winning football team or a good job, and then only until a better one comes along?

Today, committing yourself to a person for a lifetime is not considered so important. Yet many for whom it is still important, including Christians, find lifetime commitment impossible to carry out. A major reason for this is that few people learn commitment to anything in life prior to marriage. The ability to commit yourself through thick and thin doesn't come easily in marriage if you haven't learned how to work through situations in other circumstances in life.

Handling Differences the Wrong Way

What are some ways that people handle differences? One way is by giving the silent treatment. If you have a difference, you just stop communicating with the other person. You don't call, or you refuse to talk to them about the difficulty when they call. You walk by the other person as if he or she doesn't exist. This is not a recommended way. In fact, it's downright cowardly. It's even cowardly to continue the relationship, if you are avoiding the subject (or a growing list of subjects) on which you disagree. If you're going to mature as a Christian, you need to talk to the other person about your feelings and differences. I've known people who have gone months and months without knowing why another person stopped talking to them.

Some people handle differences by mocking the other person or by tearing them down and gossiping about them. Other people wouldn't think of disparaging someone else to others. Instead, they just hold a grudge. They indulge in the "I'll forgive you but I'll never forget" syndrome, which is far from biblical.

The Bible says that God not only forgives but also forgets our sins. David writes in the psalms, "As far as the east is from the west, so far has He removed our transgressions from us" (Psalm 103:12). And the prophet Micah tells us (in Micah 7:19), "Thou [God] wilt cast all their sins into the depths of the sea" (implying they will be buried too deeply ever to be found again). The prayer that the Lord taught us includes asking God to "Forgive us our debts [trespasses, sins], as we also have forgiven [others]" (Matthew 6:12). If we forgive but don't forget, then, when we pray that prayer, we are asking God to forgive but not to forget (or cleanse us of) our own sins. We need to forgive and to heal wounds and then we can consciously decide to bury the memories, just as God does, for our own sake as well as for the sake of the other person.

Accept Yourself, Then Others

An important part of learning to accept another person is learning to accept yourself first. If you don't accept yourself, you are likely to try to mold the other person into your image of the ideal partner. Unsure of yourself, you will try to convince yourself and others that your preferred way of doing things is the only correct way. Or you're likely to want the other person to have characteristics that you think you lack and need. In that way, as a couple (or as friends), you might have better status with others than you think you do as an individual.

In his book, *His Image . . . My Image*, Josh McDowell points out that a person with a weak or unhealthy self-image operates in life from factors that include:

> a view of other people as competition to beat, not friends to enjoy;
> a striving to become something or somebody, instead of relaxing and enjoying who he is;
> extreme sensitivity to the opinions of other people;
> a habit of mentally rehashing past conversations or situations, wondering what the other person meant;
> a critical and judgmental view of others; and
> a defensiveness in behavior and conversations.[1]

If any of the above fits you, then it will be hard for you to become a true friend and lover. The ability to develop a satisfying intimate relationship depends, first of all, on accepting ourselves as individuals worthy of God's love and attention. Since Christ died for us as individuals, and not only for mankind as a whole (although that is also true), then He considers us worthy enough to die for. What greater proof of our worthiness can there be than that when we come to God, He accepts us just as we are?

"For by grace you have been saved, through faith; and that not of yourselves, it is the gift of God; not as a result of works, that no one should boast" (Ephesians 2:8,9). Because He accepts us just where we are in life, we can more easily accept others where they are and we can more easily trust others to accept us the way we are. Who are we to try to force change in another person when God doesn't?

Don't misunderstand. God does expect the best from us. But when we fail (and we will), He always accepts us where we are and gives us another chance. He works with us to do better the next time with the unique abilities He has given each of us. Shouldn't we give another person the same type of freedom and encouragement?

Steps Toward Mental Intimacy

Paula and I have learned that to handle differences positively, we must *recognize, first of all, that we do have differences.* It is okay to be different. If you seem to have no differences with another person, something is wrong. There are no two people in the world exactly alike. One of you is not showing your true feelings about matters, perhaps for fear of offending or angering the other person.

Second, *appreciate the other person's opinions and ways of doing things.* The other person comes from a different background, has a different personality and different ways of doing things. Appreciate those differences as part of what makes up the total person.

Third, *endeavor to put yourself in the other person's shoes.* Try to understand that person's perspective. For some of us, this is very hard to do. We are either so talkative, so argumentative, so stubborn, or so intent on getting the other person to agree with our perspective that we never stop to think where the other person is coming from.

Fourth, *express yourself honestly.* Don't cover up your feelings with a smile, saying everything is okay when it isn't. Talk about things honestly.

Fifth, *take steps to resolve your differences.* If one solution is to break off a friendship, then that is a solution. If, however, you think you can learn to accept each other's differences and come closer to agreeing with each other's ways, then that, more likely, is a better solution.

Learning to come to a meeting of the minds — building oneness while keeping and appreciating each other's uniqueness — is a major step on the road to starring a relationship with total and balanced intimacy.

---

1. How do you normally handle differences that come up in your close relationships?

2. Which of the suggestions for how to discover what's in someone else's mind do you want to focus on and why?

3. How do you think your self-image has effected your relationships?

Chapter Ten
Understand Your Feelings

Joe was dating a really great girl and planned to marry her. One day she said, "Joseph, you're not going to believe this."

"What, Mary?"

"Ummm, well, Joseph, I'm pregnant."

"You're pregnant! Who is the guy? Where is he?"

"No, no, Joseph. You don't understand. It's God."

"God? Look, Mary, I know the facts of life. It doesn't happen like that. God doesn't do things that way!"

"I know, Joseph. . . but it's God."

"Oh, really? Well, how do you know?"

"An angel told me."

"An angel told you that it was God? Humph!"

This illustrated segment of the events surrounding the birth of Jesus puts a lot more human drama and emotion into the Christmas story than what most of us picture when we hear the following recited at Christmas time:

Now the birth of Jesus Christ was as follows. When His mother Mary had been betrothed to Joseph, before they came together she

was found to be with child by the Holy Spirit. And Joseph her
husband, being a righteous man, and not wanting to disgrace her,
desired to put her away [divorce her] secretly.

But when he had considered this, behold, an angel of the Lord
appeared to him in a dream, saying, "Joseph, son of David, do
not be afraid to take Mary as your wife; for that which has been
conceived in her is of the Holy Spirit. And she will bear a Son;
and you shall call His name Jesus, for it is He who will save His
people from their sins.

Now all this took place that what was spoken by the Lord through
the prophet might be fulfilled, saying, "Behold, the virgin shall be
with child, and shall bear a Son, and they shall call His name
Immanuel," which translated means, "God with us."

And Joseph arose from his sleep, and did as the angel of the Lord
commanded him, and took her as his wife; and kept her as a virgin
until she gave birth to a Son; and he called His name Jesus (Matthew
1:18-25).

Can't you imagine Joseph tossing and turning all night after
he first learned that Mary was pregnant? The drama that must
have been going on inside him isn't hard to comprehend. If anyone
ever wanted to believe in a virgin birth, surely it was Joseph,
even though it was contrary to all known facts. But did you ever
consider what Joseph's emotions must have been when he heard
the news that his fiancee, with whom he had never had sexual
relations, was pregnant?

Someone said to me a long time ago, "Remember, Dick,
behind every face there's a drama going on. Tap into the drama."
In relationships, we need to discover the drama going on inside
other people's lives. What is so interesting about human life is
that the drama doesn't stop. It's a never- ending saga. Therefore,
the more you tap into the drama, the more exciting life becomes.

Even in our church groups and Bible studies, I believe we
should discuss more than just who married Abraham. We should
look under the surface of biblical events and characters to find
the emotions and feelings that were going on at the time. We can
then tap into the real drama of these events, learn how biblical
characters like Joseph and Mary dealt with their feelings, and,
from that, learn more about how to lead our own lives in a godly
manner.

Sharing Feelings Is Important

You can apply this to life around you as well. When you see a person act or react, don't just look at the surface situation. Try to discover what's going on underneath the surface. How does that person feel about certain things? What makes that person feel good? What makes a person feel sad? What makes a person feel rejected?

Trying to understand the emotional makeup of the other person is neglected in most relationships. Not only is it a time-consuming task, but the other person's feelings so easily affect yours, and emotions are hard to control. As a result, perhaps most friendships develop only a lopsided star of intimacy.

Today's society gives poor advice in this area: Play it cool. Show him or her who's boss. Play hard to get. Don't show your emotions.

I disagree with this thinking completely. I believe strongly that we should expose our emotions in a relationship, not cover them up. We need to know each other's inner feelings if we are to achieve a balanced star of intimacy even though there are no easy ways to go about this.

Have you noticed that just the way you look makes some people feel rejected? Once I was eating in a romantic, candlelit restaurant with my girl friend, Lori, who suddenly asked me, "Is there anything wrong?"

"Wrong?" I responded, "nothing's wrong. Why do you ask?"

"Well, you just look like something's wrong."

"No, there's nothing wrong."

"Are you sure? You looked at me as if something were wrong."

"Well, I've got a lot on my mind."

What makes a person like Lori sense problems? What makes a person feel lonely? What makes a person feel secure or insecure? Discuss questions like these with a person who means a lot to you. Ask these same questions of yourself.

Attitudes Toward Emotions Differ

Many difficulties in a relationship stem from the different ways men and women tend to communicate. As children, boys and girls learn to communicate very differently.

Little girls open their hearts.

Girls learn a lot about interpersonal communication from playing with dolls. A girl has a cute little doll, a hunk of plastic, to which she gives a name. She says, "Baby Alice, how are you doing?" "Feed the baby mud pie." Sometimes Baby Alice gets sick and the little girl says, "Oh, my baby is sick. That's okay, Baby Alice. I'll call the doctor. Ring, ring, ring. Doctor, Baby Alice is sick. Can you come right away?" Then the little girl switches to the role of the doctor. "Oh, the baby has a broken arm. Here, I'll fix it. It won't hurt much, baby." The little girl also has a doll house with all kinds of imaginary people living in it. She learns to relate by talking to the imaginary people.

Little boys close their hearts.

And how do little boys learn to communicate? They play with toy trucks. "Vroom, vroom, vroom."
They play with toy guns. "Bang, bang, you're dead."
"I am not."
"Yes, you are."
"No, I'm not!"
In this way, little boys learn deep, caring communication. Right?
Wrong. All our lives, we men learn not to expose our hearts. We have Mom and Dad tell us, "Big boys don't cry." That isn't the truth, by the way, but our culture says it is. And as we grow up, we are taught by many people not to share our feelings. Think of the images from the media. The Clint Eastwood type. The tough guy walks into town with his machine gun and blows everyone away and then just walks on through. Can you imagine Clint Eastwood telling a woman, "I have a personal problem"?
Men watch professional football Saturday, Sunday, Monday and Thursday nights. I mean, we men love professional football. We see some of these hulks smashed to smithereens, lying on the field obliterated. But do you ever see a tear? Never. Finally, this smashed hulk will get up and hobble to the sidelines. And the whole crowd will cheer and yell for the courageous felled player. Then, as the crowd's attention returns to the field, the player will

collapse and fall apart. But not when people's attention is on him! All our lives we men learn to suck in our guts in front of other people and move on.

Emotionless Man Meets Emotional Woman

When a man comes into a relationship with a woman, he finds out that she's not like a sports coach. She wants him to show his guts. "A girl wants to know my guts? My feelings? The deep inside me?" Some of us have hidden that behind a hardened exterior, behind the successes we've strived for, for so long that we're not sure we can pull out our feelings to show them. After all, if ever we've shared our hearts with other males, they've usually joked about it (usually because they had similar emotions that they didn't want others to know about). We don't like to be mocked so we have stifled our feelings and emotions most of our lives.

Then a woman starts asking very difficult questions. Why are you upset? How do you feel about that? What do you want to do with your life? A woman wants to know a man's heart. Why? Because she wants to be a part of his life, if only for awhile, and to help him grow and develop. That's what she learned to do with her dolls and now she wants to help him with what she has learned.

But some men don't want to be helped. That's why they feel so lonely. They have stifled everything for so long that they have shriveled up inside. Deep within they know they have a sensitive heart. But they never see models of men displaying such sensitivity so they don't know how to do it.

Men Need to Share and Explain Emotions

I suggest that men take the emotional risk to begin to share what's deep down in their souls. They might be amazed how others, particularly women, will respond.

One time I was dating a really wonderful woman. It was during a time that I had been struggling about my life and career. I was an assistant pastor in a church but I didn't know what to do with my future. I knew that I didn't want to continue in that position. I wanted to be a senior pastor, but I was single and nobody wanted a single pastor. I had three or four other options but everything seemed to be failing and falling apart. I didn't know what to do.

While we were sitting in her apartment, she asked me, "Dick, what are you going to do in the future?"

I started to give her a sane, sensible reply. But suddenly my confused feelings began to come out and I began to cry. Immediately I considered this humbling and humiliating situation. If I continued to cry, she was going to reject me. I could just imagine her going back and telling her friends, "This boyfriend is a real crybaby." However, if I didn't tell her my heart and stifled everything inside again, I thought I would burst.

I had to tell somebody and she was the only one around. So I decided, "Okay, I'll open the floodgates and spill my insides. It will probably be the last time I'll see her because she'll then want to reject me. But here goes."

I told her all my fears and shared all my struggles and confusion. For a half hour, I let it pour out. When I was finished, I asked her, "What do you think about all I've said?"

I was amazed at her answer. She said, "This makes me love you all the more."

Astonished, I replied, "It does?"

I had expected rejection. What she said, in essence, was that she wanted to share in my struggles and she saw areas in which she thought she could help me.

The emotional aspect of a relationship is a very difficult one, especially for the man. He needs to learn how to communicate some of those deep inner thoughts and feelings in a relationship with a woman. Now, he doesn't need to manufacture some problem to talk about, nor does he have to cry when he tells it. But he does need to learn to share what's really important to him.

Women Need to Explain Emotions

A woman, too, has emotion-communicating problems. Usually, she doesn't mind showing her feelings. But often she thinks a man should know what her show of feelings implies without having to put it into words. Somehow, putting her emotions into words detracts from the feeling of them. She'll talk around the subject for a half hour without explaining what has caused her show of emotions, hoping he'll somehow understand. The problem is, he won't. If a woman wants to develop emotional intimacy and understanding with a man, she needs to put her feelings into words.

Without trying to discourage a woman in her desire to help with a man's burdens, I'd like to redirect the ways in which some women seek advice for this. Often, when a woman sees a problem in a man's life or a problem in their relationship with each other, she will tell her women friends about it and get their counsel for a solution. They will all have opinions. A corporate decision is then established and the woman will decide to approach the problem in that way.

She goes back to her man to try it and finds out it doesn't work! Why? Women friends have only a limited understanding of men. A woman who wants to help a man with a problem will get better advice about what to do by going to another man to get his opinion. Try it and see.

The Fear of Hurting and Being Hurt

Another area of emotions involves the fear of hurting others. Most of us don't want to bring pain into someone else's life. When we are afraid that we will hurt the other person, we keep quiet about subjects that need to be discussed. Deep inside, we may be keeping quiet for fear of getting hurt ourselves.

A person who has an overriding fear of hurting someone usually sees himself or herself in a position of power in the relationship and the other person in a position of weakness.

An overwhelming fear of hurting the other person includes a misconception of how God works in people's lives. Often God uses hurt to teach His children great lessons. But if we try to play the role of the Holy Spirit in people's lives by protecting them from hurt, we don't allow the Spirit to work.

Cindy had a lot of concerns about her boyfriend's wild past. Larry had had sexual relationships with several women before he became a Christian. Cindy's fears that he had not changed his ways kept growing. Although they were engaged, she was afraid to talk to Larry about these fears. She knew that talking about his past would be painful for him so she just swept her fears under the rug.

In reality, Cindy didn't want to discuss the situation because she might be the one to get hurt herself. She was afraid of finding out something that would harm this "dream" relationship.

Situations like this are especially devastating. The relationship, which started out in a beautiful fantasy realm, is growing, and romantic feelings get far in front of the rest of the relationship. When doubts and questions come regarding the other person's habit patterns, past, or negative qualities, we hold back from bringing these doubts into the light. After all, who wants to bring reality into Disneyland? It only takes away from the fun.

But no one can live in Disneyland for long. So a boiling cauldron of smothered emotions begins to build up underneath the surface and to shake the foundations of Disneyland. Often, one person or the other senses the uneasiness but finds it difficult to discuss openly. Both cover their fears, when what they want to do is expose and talk about them, even though this would be painful.

The Fear of Losing Control

Another fear is that of losing control. Most of us want to be the controlling factor in our own lives, including situations that involve other people. We try to make things work out the way we envision or desire because that makes us feel secure. We want to keep the upper hand in controlling a relationship.

Dating relationships reveal the insecurities in our lives. We wonder about the future. We try to avoid rejection at all costs. We worry about the other person turning on us or leaving. We hesitate to show our vulnerability and to be open with our wounds.

Cliff, for instance, has dated quite a lot of women. He once told me that he was dating a certain girl but he was getting scared. "What are you afraid of?" I asked.

"I'm afraid I'm losing control," he replied. "Previously, I've been able to have the upper hand in relationships. But I can no longer control this one. My feelings of love and my desire for commitment and marriage are getting out of hand, beyond my ability to control. I'm afraid I'm getting into an area where I can be hurt by her and hurt deeply."

Men and Vulnerability

Men are often leery of vulnerability. We are afraid to let anyone see our failures and habit patterns that are not always pleasing. To expose what we've tried to cover up for many years is very difficult.

For a man, the areas hardest to reveal involve his weaknesses. The areas of a dating relationship that are tender spots include his fears of not being a good lover and of not being able to remain committed to a partner for a lifetime. He fears intimacy, because a woman will want to know these feelings and the other issues that affect his life. So we hold back until we feel we're in much better control. We want to have all our bases covered before we get up to the plate.

I had wanted to date Barb for two years. I would see her every July at our two-week staff conference but I would never ask her out. I was too afraid that she might not like me. Finally, I worked up the courage to ask her out the following July.

I called her the first day of the conference.

"Hi, Barb!" I said. "I just arrived for the conference. Would you like to go out this evening and get something to eat?"

"I'd like to, Dick," she said, "but I'm doing some things."

So, the second day, I called her again and asked her out.

"I'd like to," she said, "but I already have some plans."

The third day was the same thing. "I'd like to, but..." Eight straight days I asked her out and got the same answer.

I will never forget the ninth day. I called her up and again asked her if she would like to go out. "I would like to," she said, "but the conference is almost over, and I'm going to be busy for the rest of it. Why don't you ask me next year?"

You know what suddenly hit me? She didn't want to go out with me! I was bothering her! I had been rejected and hadn't even realized it!

I felt so embarrassed because I hadn't picked up on her feelings sooner. You see, I had been hearing, "I would like to go out with you." But she was implying, "I will continue to have other plans." In this situation, I definitely had made myself vulnerable to hurt. But in the process I learned that I needed to be more aware and better able to pick up on what she was not saying. And Barb needed to learn how to communicate and to "tell it like it is."

The differences on the emotional level seem so simple, and yet, in life, they are so great.

Women and Loss of Direction

Often a woman is afraid of having to change her career direction for a man. Should she continue with the sense of direction she has chosen previously for her life? Or should she consider adapting her choice to a man's career direction? If she firmly believes that God led her in her present career, it may be all the harder for her. Sometimes, she keeps quiet about the dedication she has to her work goals, leaving the impression that fitting into the man's life plan would be no problem. When the relationship becomes serious, the issue finally has to be faced.

I talked with Max, a Christian businessman from Atlanta, and his girl friend, Janie, on the way to the airport. He told me repeatedly that he loved Janie and wanted her, but he felt his direction and goal in life was to become a wise businessman and to make lots of money. Janie wanted to go back to school and train to become an overseas missionary. Their different purposes created a struggle. He didn't want Janie to leave Atlanta to return to school.

Finally, Max submitted to Janie's desire and she moved away to go to school. Still, he constantly told her that she should forget her plans and become a missionary to the business world. There was struggle and manipulation between the two. Both were trying to get the other to go along with their own perspective. Both were afraid to lose the struggle, but both were also afraid to give up. They were caught in the awful middle where their relationship just muddled through. What Max and Janie needed to do was to give their relationship over to the Lord, to let Him work out whatever He wanted for their relationship and for each of them individually.

The Fear of Failure

Of course, giving the relationship over to the Lord is hard to do when you have to consider the possible failure of the relationship. Each may have had other relationships that have broken up or they have seen those of friends or relatives end painfully. They don't want this one to fail, so any inkling of failure is cause for great concern. When the going gets tough, they try harder and harder. Sometimes by working harder, the relationship becomes more strained. Meanwhile, both people lose the joy and spontaneity they originally had with each other.

When you put so much time into a relationship getting to know another person, you don't want to say goodbye because then you have to start all over with someone else. Or, what may seem even worse, you see no one on the horizon with whom to start over. Many times a person hangs onto another just for security, even though the relationship isn't going anywhere. Sometimes a couple keeps dating for years because one person is clinging emotionally to the other for security. Deep down inside, each is afraid to admit that the relationship may be over or that there needs to be some sort of confrontation.

How to Achieve Emotional Closeness

The emotional area is such a sensitive one because you are a sensitive being. You want to be loved and to love, to belong to someone. There is a great urge within you to knock down the walls of secrecy and to reveal the deep-down-inside you. If you realize that the special person in your life wants the same thing, it helps you to let the deep-down-inside you be seen. Building understanding between our feelings and sensitivities is a long, sometimes tortuous road, but it is well worth the effort.

1. Learn to observe.

Observe what a person likes or dislikes. Pick up non-verbal signs, such as a frown, a slammed door, a sudden silence or a swift change of subject. Then communicating simple curiosity, ask for the reason behind the action. Observe how a person relates with other people. Observe what depresses them and what encourages them. Relate to them on those issues.

Men, you will be amazed that, to women, such thoughtfulness will go a long way. We men think that when we ask a girl out for a date, all we have to do to make it a fantastic time is spend a lot of money. Sometimes women are more interested in simpler things, just talking and relating. That usually doesn't excite a man much because he doesn't know what to talk about. However, by using the key words learned in the last chapter — who, what, why, where, when, how, and explain — the two of you can learn a lot about each other's feelings.

2. Realize it is normal to have fears of vulnerability.

We don't like to fail or to lose control. Relationships are a risk. We have a tendency to hold back and to let the other person take the initiative. Don't wait for your friend to start the discussion. Talk about your real self and ask questions to stimulate further transparency between you.

If the other person doesn't want to talk about something, however, immediately back off. Give the person emotional space. Timing is an important part of building emotional intimacy.

After I finish a speech, I am sensitive to criticism. I've given it my best shot and I hope the audience has responded favorably. Paula has come to realize that the best time to help me improve my talks is a few hours after I have finished or the next day. By then I have calmed down and can look at the talk more objectively. Paula then discusses with me its positive and negative factors and encourages me to become more effective. She has learned when to interact and when it's better to be silent.

3. Build an emotional refuge in your relationships.

The world batters us and degrades our humanity. Intimate friendships should provide a refuge from the attacks of society.

You should feel free enough with each other to discuss the full range of your feelings, both positive and negative. Don't hide behind an "off limits" sign. Learn to accept each other for the real people you are.

A word of warning in this regard. One of the worst mistakes you can make after someone has expressed his or her true feelings to you is to tell other friends all the details. Nothing angers a person more than to hear that something told in trust has become common knowledge. A confidence has been betrayed. The hurt will cause the other person to withdraw from you emotionally. Private conversations are private knowledge. Build trust in each other. That encourages further sharing and openness. Scripture says, "Bear one another's burdens, and thus fulfill the law of Christ" (Galations 6:2).

4. Channel your emotions.

At the beginning of a relationship, don't let strong emotions build too fast. Too many couples get overly excited at the start of their relationship. When they meet someone who makes the heart pound wildly, they spend many hours together, day after day. They can't get enough of each other. This may be "the one!"

Then reality descends. Each one notices things about the other that are disturbing. They get tired of being together so much. They don't want to acknowledge this for fear the other person will take it in the wrong way and break up.

Don't allow this kind of pressure to destroy a potentially good relationship. You may be indulging in too much talk about "us and the future." If your relationship becomes over-analyzed, the fun will be lost and it will become drudgery.

Back up in your emotional intensity. Give each other some freedom to be alone or to be with other friends. For awhile, put a moratorium on serious conversations about where your relationship is headed. Emphasize mutual understanding, honesty and enjoyment. Allow time for slower, more solid growth. Be yourself and, if the person doesn't like who you are, that's a sure sign that person is not the one for you. Part on friendly terms, respecting each other's uniqueness and personality.

5. Balance your heart and your head.

We have a tendency to go too much toward one extreme or the other. You don't want to become either an emotional basket case or an unfeeling machine. You need the balanced combination of emotions and reason, of love and truth. Neither should totally rule you. Listen to your heart and listen to your head. If they are not saying the same thing, don't make any major decisions or commitments. Wait until both your head and your heart say similar things.

It is okay to communicate your doubts about your relationship, as well as your certainties. Honesty allows each of you to know where both of you stand.

Often relationships end up in the *yo-yo syndrome.* As a person playing with two yo-yos can never get them to be in the same place at the same time, often a couple faces this situation in their emotions. While one is thinking this friendship is wonderful, the other is feeling uneasy about it. After awhile the reverse may be true. The person who used to be uneasy warms up to the other and the person who was excited about the two of them cools down.

Ask Christ to get the yo-yo emotions coordinated, one way or the other. Don't pressure the other person to be where you are emotionally. Be patient and allow time for change. Too often we are in a rush and end up driving the other person away.

In learning emotional closeness, give freedom to each other to feel personal feelings and to confront personal doubts.

6. Seek to encourage the other person.

Ask God for wisdom regarding the other person's life. What are some of his or her needs? A good question to ask someone you are dating is, "What is your most important need today? And how can I help you with it?" Now, you can't fill every need, but if your intention is to help that person mature emotionally, he or she may respond and may also help you out later.

7. Learn to be positive around others.

A negative attitude affects the other person's emotions. Think of good things that can happen. If the other person is discouraged, recognize their discouragement or other negative feelings, then together consider what God is likely to do to remedy the situation.

Emotional closeness involves not only sharing emotions, but empathizing with each other, and then helping the overburdened person find a way up toward more positive outlooks and emotions. As the wise King Solomon said, in Ecclesiastes 4:9,10, "Two are better than one.... For if either of them falls, the one will lift up his companion."

---

1. What aspects of sharing yourself emotionally are the most difficult for you?

2. What do you expect to gain emotionally from your relationships with someone of the other sex?

3. What positive steps can you take to develop your relationships further in this area?

Chapter Eleven
Express Love Creatively

SOCIAL

MENTAL

THE
PHYSICAL

EMOTIONAL

Peggy, a single woman, has been in the Christian ministry for years. During most of that time her friends and dates were in full-time Christian work, too. After spending much of her ministry traveling, she finally settled in a major southern city and became active in the singles group of a large church. The people in the group were from the ordinary working world. They shared Peggy's beliefs and viewpoints about Christ and Christianity.

Because of this, Peggy was flabbergasted when she found how many of the men wanted to get involved sexually on a first or second date. In fact, she discovered that a number of them had been sexually active already with other women in the group. She was shocked to realize that so many Christians would be involved in these practices.

Peggy shouldn't have been shocked. Everything we read and hear today — songs on the radio, TV programs, movies — all express that sexual closeness is the "ultimate" experience that everyone is searching for. A minister to a singles church group has said that 70 percent of the singles who come to him for counsel are sexually active.

John, another friend of mine, dated Elaine for quite awhile. She told him that she wanted to stay completely away from the physical side of a relationship. John was impressed and respected her for her stand. They had no physical involvement whatsoever during their courtship and didn't even talk about it. They did pray, however, about whether or not they were meant for each other and felt that God was leading them together.

After they married, John discovered that Elaine's desire for no physical contact before marriage wasn't primarily to remain pure. She just had no interest in sex. In fact, she thought sex was dirty. Consequently, they have had tremendous problems in their marriage.

The above examples are just some of the physical and sexual dilemmas that Christian singles encounter today.

The initial interest in a person usually involves a sexual attraction but that interest must broaden to include the whole person if the relationship is to be meaningful, beneficial and satisfying. In today's world, outside deterrents to sexual experience before marriage (the fear of pregnancy; society's disapproval; and family, friends, and neighbors who were aware of your daily actions) have been replaced by birth control, a society and peers who encourage sexual experience, and uncaring and unknown neighbors. All of these make it hard to know how to find and build a relationship and still keep within God's commandments for sex and marriage.

The Fireworks Pattern

There are two extremes in the physical area of dating that I believe should be avoided. The first is called the "fireworks pattern." Peggy encountered this pattern in the church singles group she attended. This is where a man and woman meet each other and it's like electricity. Perhaps they've known each other casually for awhile before, perhaps not. Because they can talk a long time about many subjects, especially if they know Christ and can talk about Christian things, the energy just naturally flows. There is a flood of emotion and of exhiliration in their hearts. They become interested in each other physically and their expectations are immediate. Very soon there is an intense desire to get involved sexually.

At times like this, it is hard to remember that premarital sex is strictly forbidden by God, not once, but many times in the

Bible. Such verses as 1 Corinthians 6:9,10, Galatians 5:19-21, Ephesians 5:3-5, Colossians 3:5, 1 Thessalonians 4:3,4 and Hebrews 13:4 all speak against sex outside marriage.

Why must sex wait until marriage? Because God values you so very much as a person. When you have been deeply involved with someone else through physical intimacies and intercourse, you have given something of your life away that you can never give again. You can give away your virginity to only one person. Then, if that sexual partner leaves your life physically or emotionally, something of you goes too. That's why you build a wall around your heart to protect what's left of it.

Several words in the Bible are used to describe sexual immorality. One is the word *adultery*. Most people believe this word refers to one or both people in a sexual situation being married to someone else. However, the biblical word is more general than that. It can mean either premarital or extramarital sex, immorality, or promiscuity. In the Bible, adultery often refers to premarital sexual contact whether either party is married to someone else or not. It is used a number of ways in the New Testament but it always means sexual intercourse outside the marriage bonds.

The word *fornication* usually refers to sex with someone who is not married. This could mean either one or both of the people are not married. Some of the strongest statements in the Bible are against fornication. It is never right under any circumstances, even if the couple is in love and planning to marry.

God makes this very clear in 1 Corinthians 6. Verses 9 and 10 say: "Do you not know that the unrighteous shall not inherit the Kingdom of God? Do not be deceived; neither fornicators, nor idolators, nor adulterers, nor effeminate [by perversion], nor homosexuals, nor thieves, nor the covetous, nor drunkards, nor revilers, nor swindlers, shall inherit the kingdom of God."

This statement leaves no room for excuses and rationalizations. The very next verse, however, holds out hope. "And such were some of you; but you were washed; but you were sanctified, but you were justified in the name of the Lord Jesus Christ, and in the Spirit of our God" (1 Corinthians 6:11). In other words, none of these wrongdoers will inherit the kingdom of God, unless they have been forgiven by God. Many of the people of the church at

Corinth had participated in one or more of these actions. But when they sought God's forgiveness for their evil ways, He accepted them and changed their lives, gave them salvation and sanctified them (made them holy and separated them from the world for His service).

These verses show that any type of immorality, premarital or extra- marital sex, is wrong. God, in essence, says, "I don't want that to be part of your life, period." These warnings are established by God to prevent humanity, those created in His image, from becoming like animals. Sex is far more important to human beings, God's highest creation, than just a physical activity. Sex is a wonderful activity — a relationship of total commitment — but it is in the context of marriage that this full coming together of a man and a woman is to be developed.

For those who have given away their virginity and wish they hadn't, there is still hope for the future. God can cleanse you of past sin — emotionally, mentally and spiritually. You can start on a new track of sexual purity and reserve yourself from now on for that special person to come into your life. You can never be a physical virgin again. However, if God has cleansed you, you can develop emotional virginity that you can keep and then give away when God leads you into a lifetime marital commitment.

The "Nothing Until Marriage" Pattern

While keeping your virginity for marriage, there is another extreme to consider in the physical area of dating relationships. Some Christians believe in the "nothing until marriage" pattern. Having had previous difficulties in relationships, they now want to avoid any physical contact with the other sex altogether. They decide that they will not kiss another person until the wedding ceremony.

Some people would call this viewpoint admirable. But as we have already seen with John and Elaine, this too can present problems. It can put too much pressure and emphasis on the other areas of a relationship, especially on the spiritual. Only through prayer can they have any sensitivity that the other person is for them. Some very spiritual Christians would say amen to that, but few of use are that spiritual. We don't always know God's leading correctly without circumstances also being a factor in His guidance.

In the area of relationships, guidance through circumstances does involve physical attraction and response to each other's touch. It is difficult, however, to consider the "fireworks pattern" of attraction and response as evidence of God's leading because it is likely to burn itself out.

Total abstinence of any physical contact may be spiritually motivated. It may present fewer problems than the "sexual fireworks" pattern since it avoids the immorality and possible heartbreak of premarital sex. However, no physical contact, even through the engagement period, is not only unrealistic but stifling.

I believe there needs to be a balance for the physical area. The physical aspect of a relationship is not only an important and critical part of developing togetherness, but also it must parallel the degree of commitment that both people have to the relationship using the biblical guidelines explained later in this chapter. And both parties should understand what meaning each of them gives to their affection.

Men Communicate Physically

Men often communicate more physically than verbally. If a man likes another man, what does he do? He slugs him on the back. If he really likes him, he wrestles him and nearly breaks his arm! That shows real care and love. We men are very competitive physically and like challenges. If a line is set that we're not supposed to cross, we're going to try to cross it. If a woman sets a sexual boundary, a man will want to try to break it.

When it comes to a relationship, men tend to get physical too fast. It comes from the way they face other things in life. When a woman challenges a man by her high moral standards, often it will tend to spur him on even harder — even if it means marrying her in order to get to her sexually. This is why God must be the one to control the boundaries and drives that entice men.

In *The Social Control of Sexuality*, John Delamater states that adolescent males approach sexual behavior from a recreational perspective. Often they are interested in the pleasure it brings and the status it gives them with their peers. Females approach sexuality with a relational perspective. They view it within the context of commitment, falling in love and marriage. As a man gets older, he seeks greater companionship and intimacy. But, for men, these are still sought through physical interaction.₁

Women Communicate Emotionally

Women, on the other hand, communicate more emotionally. Men may give away their physical being too fast, but women are likely to give away their heart too fast. Women often dream and fantasize, not so much about what it would be like to have sex with a man they've just met, but what it would be like to experience romantic tenderness and closeness with him, usually within the context of marriage and family life.

From the very onset of physical involvement, both the man and woman need to know where the other is coming from. That first kiss may have different meanings to each of them. Have you ever, either before or after kissing, asked a date what a kiss means to him or her? Probably not. It seems presumptuous and might be embarrassing to find out. Nevertheless, you need to know beforehand what a kiss is likely to mean to the other person.

I say to men, "Learn to say I love you without sexual intimacies involved. Learn to be a lover in the true sense of the word. Learn to love with your soul." The apostle Paul said, "Having thus a fond affection for you, we were well pleased to impart to you not only the gospel but also our lives, because you had become very dear to us" (1 Thessalonians 2:8). Learn to give your soul to people, and particularly to the other sex as you develop a caring relationship. Learn to give your heart away. We men sit behind a wall too often. We need to be more verbal and more expressive.

Women relate to feelings. Many a man has had a woman pick up on his feelings before he knows what they are himself. A woman can tell when he's down when he doesn't know it or when he doesn't want the woman to know it. The closer you get to a woman emotionally, the more she picks up on these feelings.

Often a woman will come on too strong about a man's emotions, always asking, "What's wrong, what's wrong?" The man doesn't know himself. His answer may be, "I don't know. I don't even care. All I want to do is live. Leave me alone!" Sometimes women need to slow down the process of asking deeply penetrating questions. Instead, learn to pray that God will encourage a man to open up his heart to you. Ask God for internal motivation for that man. Be careful, however, not to manipulate, not to rearrange things to control a man or to get what you want from his inner soul.

Learn to Love Non-Physically

When Paula and I started dating, I wanted to develop a caring for her. Although I wasn't in love with her at the time, it seemed the natural thing to do to express this caring physically. From the experience of previous relationships, I wanted to put my arm around her, kiss her and hold her close.

Whenever I would get close to her in the car, however, I noticed that she would become quiet and seemingly disinterested. One night she sensed that I was going to put my arm around her and try to kiss her. She then told me that she had been thinking about this possibility awhile and wanted to talk. For both of us, it was embarrassing to bring up physical desires in conversation.

As she searched for the right words, she told me that she was having a lot of fun in our dating relationship and thoroughly enjoyed being with me. "But I've learned lessons from previous dating," she said. "I care for you but, at this point, I really don't want to become involved romantically. I would appreciate it if you didn't kiss me or hold my hand, because if you do I'm afraid my heart will get easily confused. I have a tendency to let my heart get ahead of my head.

"I was in another relationship," she continued, "where we developed the romantic side of the relationship too quickly. When we broke up, I realized that I did not really love him. I had only wanted closeness. So I would appreciate it if we didn't kiss or even hold hands until we are much closer to developing a committed relationship."

You can imagine my reaction. I was frustrated and upset. How else was I going to express my caring for her? I thought it was impossible! I went home that night and told God that I couldn't do it. I had to have some physical activity. I was angry. For two days I simmered about the idea of not being able to hold her hand or kiss her.

As I prayed about it, however, I realized that my attention was in the wrong place. I was centering on the sacrifices that I was making, rather than on building up Paula, giving to her and meeting her particular desires and needs. So I decided to do what she had asked. Unless and until we had a deeper, committed relationship, I would not hold her hand or kiss her. You talk about needing the power of God. I really did.

To my amazement, it soon became exciting to realize how I could develop other areas of our relationship. This stipulation forced me to think how I could love Paula and show her, without physical contact, that I cared for her. It took a lot of creativity but, as a result, our relationship really blossomed.

In previous relationships, I often would get myself into trouble. It was easy for me to get physical too fast and then feel discouraged about the relationship ever working out. Then either the girl or I would break it off.

This time was unique and new. I was going to allow God to use each of us to show the other how to love creatively. If there was any possibility of our getting together, I wanted her to understand from her heart, her head, her spirit and every other aspect of her person that I was the one. At this point, I didn't know if I was the one, but I certainly wanted to find out.

Communicate the Meaning of Touching

As the level of commitment grows toward engagement and marriage, there should be some development of affection. But both persons need to know what that development means to the other. Of course, God always reserves physical intercourse for marriage — when you are in the bonds of Christ and of each other. Yet physical affection is a wonderful thing in a dating relationship. To touch, to hug, to run your fingers through the other's hair, to pat the other person on the back — these are all wonderful signs of affection. We should have controlled freedom, but not license, to love creatively under God.

Women enjoy physical contact and touching with a man they like and enjoy. It can't be forced or superficial. Often, however, men misinterpret an openness to closeness and body contact from a woman as an invitation to have sexual contact. This is why each person needs to communicate thoughts and feelings to the other, and then focus on the non-sexual closeness, companionship and friendship that they share. As Romans 12:9 says, "Let your affection be without hypocrisy."

God's Principles for Loving

While the Bible says that sexual intercourse is to be confined to marriage, we still have the question, "How far do you go?" Yes, we should not have premarital sex, but how close to it can we get?

Singles in Bible times didn't have these problems. In those days, Mom and Dad often chose a mate for the children; many times, the bride and groom never met until they married. Needless to say, there was very little physical contact of any kind prior to marriage. (Of course, even back then, there were prostitutes, but ordinary people had very little physical contact with the opposite sex before they married.)

The Scriptures don't specifically address our modern-day problems of how far dating partners can go in physical intimacies, except to say that you shouldn't have intercourse before marriage. So we have to look at scriptural principles to help us determine correct sexual conduct as a single person.

Principle 1: Don't let anything dominate you.

All things are lawful for me, but not all things are profitable. All things are lawful for me, but I will not be mastered by anything (1 Corinthians 6:12).

Now this verse is part of an exhortation referring specifically to sexual conduct. "Everything is lawful, but don't let anything dominate you." So, nothing, especially physical intimacy, that begins to usurp your attention and your habit patterns should take over your life. A Christian should not let anything but Christ dominate his or her life.

Sexual attraction is the strongest drive we have outside of the survival drives (food, sleep and shelter). Therefore, it is like opening Pandora's box. When you begin to experience some sexual intimacies, it lets a lot of other things come into your life and you can hardly close that box again.

Lust refers to a natural drive gone wild. When you start to get involved with heavy kissing and petting, your mind goes on ahead and begins to fantasize. Not only while you're with the person, but all the time. Sexual fantasizing takes over your mind, wherever you are, whatever you're doing. Pretty soon, the activities of a date are only a preliminary for the final activity in the back seat of the car or on the living room couch.

Did you ever notice that the more you make out, the less you talk? When you first start dating someone you talk a lot, but the more you make out on a date, the more shallow your verbal communication becomes and the more lopsided your star of intimacy is. If lusting is becoming habitual in your thinking, acting, and reacting on dates, and you're talking less, then beware. As far as God is concerned, that is a big red flag. Christians should not come under the domination of anything except Jesus Christ.

Principle 2: Acknowledge your identification with Christ.

Food is for the stomach, and the stomach is for food; but God will do away with both of them. Yet the body is not for immorality, but for the Lord; and the Lord is for the body. Now God has not only raised the Lord, but will also raise us up through His power. Do you not know that your bodies are members of Christ? Shall I then take away the members of Christ and make them members of a harlot [promiscuous woman]? May it never be! (1 Corinthians 6:13-15).

Paul is saying that you are a member of Christ and Christ is a member of you. There is a oneness. We are identified with Jesus Christ. So, when you become involved in sexual intimacies, Jesus Christ is right there, too. Whether you want to believe it or not, you are bringing Christ into that immoral activity. The Lord is for the body, and the body is for the Lord.

When you go on a date and know you are going to really make out, where do you usually want God? At home. Or, at least, in the trunk of the car. Yet, when two Christians bring their bodies together, God is right there with them.

The greatest emotional high is to come together with your wife or husband in marriage and to know what God smiles on that because He has brought two people together and made them one flesh. That is why, when we go too far sexually before marriage, we try to cover up. We don't want God to be around. Have you ever played Christian music during a passionate make-out? Acknowledging before we go on a date that our bodies are the Lord's will really cause us to think.

Principle 3: Flee Immorality.

> Or do you not know that the one who joins himself to a harlot is one body with her. For He says, "The two will become one flesh." But the one who joins himself to the Lord is one spirit with Him. Flee immorality. Every other sin that a man commits is outside the body, but the immoral man sins against his own body (1 Corinthians 6:16-18).

When we sin in sexual immorality, we harm our own bodies. I don't know all that that means, but let's consider some of its meaning.

First, we risk venereal disease. Recently a woman working in Christian ministry came to me and said that she had been sexually involved with a man and now has venereal disease. It will be with her the rest of her life. Venereal disease ravages the body. No bodily function is safe from its attack.

Second, we develop habit patterns. When a person leaves your life, you still keep the habit pattern of sexual immorality which is likely to be carried over to the next person you date.

Third, we get excited about the forbidden. As your body gets turned on from the excitement of the forbidden, what happens when you get married? The excitement leaves. One of the greatest problems in marriage today is boredom with sex. The more you mess around with sex before marriage, the less exciting it is after the wedding. Before marriage, your body reacts excitedly to the forbidden aspect of sex. When you marry and take the "forbidden fruits" idea out of sex and heavy petting, you take out much of the excitement. You've conditioned yourself to look for the wrong kind of excitement in sex.

Principle 4: Glorify God in your body.

Or do you not know that your body is a temple of the Holy
Spirit who is in you, whom you have from God, and that
you are not your own? For you have been bought with a
price: therefore glorify God in your body (1 Corinthians
6:19,20).

Now, again, I don't totally understand what "glorify God in
your body" means. But it does include the idea of doing holy
things — things that edify and build up.

When you lust a lot or are involved in premarital petting and
sexual intimacies, you feel guilty and, the more you become
involved, the colder you get toward God. You don't want to read
the Bible. You rationalize your activities. You don't want to be
around God because He sees what you are doing in a different
way from the way you want to look at it. You also get cold toward
other believers, those who are smiling and singing about God.
Who wants to smile when you feel guilty? Pre-marital sexual
involvement drives you further from the star of total intimacy
instead of bringing you closer to it.

In college, when we were talking about this idea, a girl told
me, "When I get married and have sex with my husband, I want
to be able to pray at the same time." Think about that. Seriously.
Just to have the smile of God on a relationship and to know that
He is right there is worth the world. There is no hiding. The
relationship is free and open before Him.

Principle 5: Choose honorable activities.

For this is the will of God, your sanctification [which means
to make you holy or set apart for Him]; that is, that you
abstain from sexual immorality; that each of you know how
to possess his own vessel [his own body] in sanctification
and honor, not in lustful passion, like the Gentiles [non-Chris-
tians] who do not know God (1 Thessalonians 4:3-5).

So, Paul says, choose activities that are wholesome and honorable. That is, don't participate in things where you can start
losing control.

Principle 6: *Don't defraud.*

And that no man transgress or defraud his brother in the matter because the Lord is the avenger in all these things, just as we also told you before and solemnly warned you. For God has not called us for the purpose of impurity, but in sanctification. Consequently, he who rejects this is not rejecting man but the God who gives His Holy Spirit to you (1 Thessalonians 4:6-8).

This is a major principle. The word *defraud* means to inflame someone's passions without being able to righteously fulfill them. In essence, you are giving the other person a false lead. Our bodies are designed somewhat like the transmission of a car. That is, when you start up a car, you put it into first gear. When you speed up, it wants to go into second, then third and fourth. The car is so designed that, when you start up the process, it wants to go to its conclusion. This is a natural process with the body. God designed foreplay to lead to intercourse. When you start foreplay, your mind and body naturally start going forward toward the conclusion of the sexual act. Defrauding means to get the engine going inside of you (or the other person) without intending to travel to your destination.

A question being asked today by those who want to follow biblical commands and yet are caught up in the current emphasis on sexual freedom is, "What is intercourse?" After one of my meetings, Jeff asked me if intercourse had to include physical penetration. In other words, he wanted to know if it was all right for Christians to become involved in anything that did not include physical penetration of a man into a woman.

Jesus Christ put thinking like this on a different level. In Matthew 5:27 and 28, He said, "You have heard that it was said, 'You shall not commit adultery;' but I say to you, that everyone who looks on a woman to lust for her has committed adultery with her already in his heart." It is not only the physical act, but the mental images that come to mind that are wrong. Christ took the emphasis away from just the physical and put it into the realm of the mental activity that occurs before the physical.

When Jeff told me that he could lie naked with his girl friend and not have intercourse, I knew he had gone beyond God's guidelines. Unless we are married and desire to complete the sexual act with our marriage partner, lying naked with one another must fall in the realm of defrauding.

If you have a hard time in the area of defrauding, then don't start up the engine. What starts up your engine? Holding hands? French kissing? Fondling? Whatever gets you going, stop the internal motor before you go too far.

Some ask, who should stop the process, the man or the woman? If you have trouble in this area, why don't the two of you seek God's direction together before you start up your engines? Seek His guidance as to what you should do and how you should behave.

Did you ever notice that when you're involved with someone, you want to have sex, but you don't want to? You like it, but you don't like it. When you get to the point where there is confusion, emptiness, frustration or guilt, you are beginning to defraud. The number one reason why couples break up is that they have become too close sexually before marriage.

Principle 7: Avoid tempting situations.

Flee from youthful lusts, and pursue after righteousness, faith, love and peace (2 Timothy 2:22).

If your desire is leading into areas you believe you should not get into, then get out of there immediately. Don't stay there and think, *I know I've got to get out of this situation soon.* Don't wait for soon. Do it now!

There's the old analogy about putting a frog in a pot of water. Put it in when the pot is boiling and the frog jumps right back out again. Put it in when the water is cold, and he'll enjoy it. Then turn up the heat ever so slowly and the frog will stay in the water, relaxing in its warmth. He will stay in the pot until he boils to death.

It's the same way with sexual intimacies. Don't wait to stop until you feel you're reaching the point of no return. Better yet, don't get in the pot even when the water is cold. Find out what constitutes the pot for you and find some functional substitutes. Some suggestions for functional substitutes are:

1) Don't spend time talking on the living room sofa; sit around the kitchen table instead.

2) Don't park the car in a dark, lonely spot. Buy something to drink (it helps to have something else to do with your hands) and pull into a well-lighted and busy parking lot. Watching the people go by also helps to break the pull of intense physical attraction.
3) If both the above are still too tempting, spend your talking time at a friend or relative's home, at a restaurant or ice cream shop or the eating area of a late-night supermarket.

You're right, these places aren't romantic. That's the idea! Remember, if you marry this person, most of your time with him or her will be in an unromantic environment. If you wonder how you would respond to your dating partner in the everyday circumstances of married life, then these functional substitutes will help provide an answer.

If you have had problems in the area of physical intimacy before, tell the Lord that you have learned your lesson. Accept His forgiveness and trust Him for His power to lead a holy life.

Handling Your Sexual Desires

Where do you start to control your feelings toward another person?

1. Admit you have sex drives.

If you have no current love interest, you sometimes try to deny your drives. All the time, you know you're a roaring lion underneath.

Be encouraged. God is the one who gives us an interest in the other sex. Why deny or ask Him to remove His God-given interests? However, remember there is a difference between interest and lust. Now, I think the greatest creation of God is a woman. I don't know of anything that rivals her for first place. But you can appreciate the other sex without lusting.

2. Submit your sexual desires to God.

Keep giving them to the Lord. Christ said the greatest commandments are to love the Lord your God with all your heart, soul, and mind and to love your neighbor as yourself (see Matthew 22:36,39). When you can't fulfill your sexual desire, then love God more. Have a passion for Jesus Christ, a humility before Him, since He is the only one who can give you control.

> Discipline yourself for the purpose of godliness... [which] is profitable for all things, since it holds promise for the present life and also for the life to come (1 Timothy 4:7,8).

So turn over your desires to the Lord and ask Him for the power and the courage to control your passions.

3. Keep your mind pure.

> Finally, brethren, whatever is true, whatever is honorable, whatever is right, whatever is pure, whatever is lovely, whatever is of good repute [reputation], if there is any excellence and if anything worthy of praise, let your mind dwell on these things (Philippians 4:8).

The conversations you have, the magazine pictures you look at and the TV programs you watch may have a tendency to inflame your mind. When you inflame your mind with all the sexuality and sensuality of the world, it's no wonder you have problems. Remember this, you are the only guardian of your mind. No one else is going to protect you. Fill your mind with Scripture and wholesome things.

4. Channel your energies.

Let God channel this deep-seated power of wanting somebody toward a desire to help other people. This is what kept me going for many years. Take opportunities to give to all kinds of people.

5. Develop friendships with the other sex.

Sometimes, if you're not dating, all you want to do is talk to someone of the other sex. You want to know something about how the other half of the world lives. Aren't they a mystery?

I say again, begin to develop good, deep friendships with people of the other sex. Don't limit this to people you are interested in romantically, but include people who can be good, dependable friends. Take the initiative to be friendly. When you are lonely, the tendency is to withdraw. Do the opposite. Get a group of people together and have a fun time.

6. Build a support group.

Start a CELL (Christians Encouraging, Loving, Learning) group. Get a group of men (or women, if you're a woman) with whom you really want to become blood brothers or sisters. Pour your souls out together. Uphold each other in prayer. The Bible says to bear one another's burdens (Galatians 6:2). But in order to do that, you must know what another person's burdens are.

What Tunes Your Life?

Sex is similar to the tuning of an orchestra. In a symphony orchestra, you have many fine, delicate instruments. You have the woodwinds — the oboe, the clarinet, the flute and the bassoon. You have the stringed instruments — violins, violas and cellos. You have the brass — trumpets, trombones and French horns. You have the percussion — tympani, bells and bass drum. If you're playing "The Overture of 1812," you also have a few cannons on stage.

You usually tune an orchestra through the first violin. As the first violinist tunes and then repeatedly plucks an *A*, the whole orchestra tunes their instruments to that same tone. But what if the tympani or the bass drum players decide they don't want to be tuned that way? They want to tune the orchestra. The bass drum would break out in tremendous booms that would drown out all those delicate instruments.

Sex is similar to that. It is one of the greatest drives in our lives. Once we become involved in it, it has the tendency to overpower all those fine, delicate areas involved in our star of intimacy that we already have talked about — the social, mental, spiritual, and emotional areas of life.

We have to realize that the physical area of a relationship needs to be in coordination with the other areas of our lives and, in particular, with the level of commitment of the other individual in the relationship. The level of commitment is critically important.

So remember to enjoy the other person, to bear each other's burdens, to pursue godliness and always to walk with the King (Jesus).

---

1. What physical difficulties do you run into?

2. What gets your engine going?

3. How do you handle your sexual desires?

Chapter Twelve
Explore Your Souls

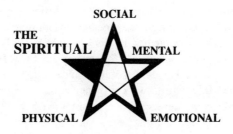

When Paula and I were in Paris we visited Le Louvre Museum and spent hours looking at its beautiful art objects. A large crowd of people stood in front of one painting, blocking our view. As people moved on, we got closer and saw that the painting was the famous Mona Lisa. We had seen copies in books and magazines, but here was the original, the masterpiece created by Leonardo da Vinci. We stood captivated by its beauty and elegance.

God is an artist and originator, too, greater than da Vinci. God is the creative genius not only of the material world but also of relationships. Even in the Garden of Eden God said about Adam, "It is not good for man to be alone" (Genesis 2:18). He decided to create Eve, so that Adam could have a companion and a deep oneness with another being like himself.

As the architect of relationships, God knows all the intricacies in building a beautiful original. Far more than just giving us an original to copy, He has given us guidelines for developing our own original relationships, ones that will satisfy us for a lifetime.

Spiritual Goals for Dating

A good marriage is built upon the habits and character that each person develops before marriage. The quality of a dating relationship, and later a marriage, depends upon the quality of each person's personal life and spiritual walk with Jesus Christ.

In the Scriptures, God gives us His beautiful, original design for the marriage relationship, the ultimate in intimate relating. This design portrays the functioning of a husband and a wife in a tight-knit unit. As we study the original design we can see how to build a dating relationship into one of close intimate commitment.

God gives us a quality in our associations with others that we can never give ourselves. To accomplish this, He has given the Holy Spirit as helper, assistant, guide and source of power. Without the Holy Spirit, we could never develop anything close to what God has to offer us. He is the master teacher of relationships.

We must admit that marriage is in trouble today. The growing rate of divorce, numbers of abused wives and children, and increase in unhappiness, loneliness and frustration all show that to be true. This is not because God's original design is wrong, but because human copies and imitations of it are nowhere near what God intended for us.

Many different ideas about relationships are espoused by books, movies, television, etc. Recently a famous movie star appeared on television explaining the joy of having a baby outside of marriage. She had lived with her lover, the father of her child, for five years, but still she didn't plan to marry him. Such ideas broadcast widely by the media affect many people's lives. They say, "Well, if that star can do it, then I can too." Yet years later, we will see the wreckage of this type of relationship.

Down through the ages when people have said, "I have a better way; I know how to build a better relationship," they inevitably have found out differently. Anything but God's design is a cheap imitation.

In years past, children were reared in the Judeo/Christian principles of living, which included relationships. By the time a person married, they knew how to build, if not the best, at least a solid marriage relationship. Today, when ungodly ideals permeate our society and world, perhaps most people, even Christian singles, have not learned before marriage how to build a marriage relationship.

Walking down the aisle at the wedding ceremony does not change habits or character to good marriage traits. Before marriage is the time to build the qualities that will foster a good relationship, not just for one or two years, but for a lifetime.

Dating Goal 1: Building Unity

Right after God created Eve, He told Adam, "For this cause a man shall leave his father and his mother, and shall cleave to his wife; and they shall become one flesh" (Genesis 2:24). When Christ was on earth, He quoted that verse and then added these words to it, "Consequently they are no more two, but one flesh. What therefore God has joined together, let no man separate" (Matthew 19:6).

The first aspect of married unity is to *leave*. You leave your parents or anyone else on whom you've been dependent for emotional, mental, or material needs or guidance. Regarding parents, you're called upon to love, honor and respect them; but when you marry, you are to leave dependency on them or others behind, and learn to depend upon and be responsible to your mate. Dependency on parents and relatives can be a major problem of newly married couples. Certainly it is proper to seek the friendship and counsel of others outside the marriage, but the final decisions should be made between the marriage partners who now take responsibility for their own lives together.

The second aspect of unity is to *cleave* to each other in marriage. This word means to stick like glue. If, when you walk down the aisle at your wedding ceremony, you do it with the attitude, "I hope this works," I guarantee you that it won't work. Too many complications and difficulties come into any marriage that would disintegrate it, if you hold only to a "hope so" attitude.

When speaking at a large high school convention, I mentioned that when Paula and I married, I told her, "Honey, the only thing that will separate us is death; either you will die or I will die." Suddenly, nine hundred students erupted in applause and cheering. This shocked me. Apparently, many of them came from broken or loveless homes. What these kids desired deep in their souls was a strong family relationship where mother and father deeply loved each other and were cleaving to each other through thick and thin, in good times and bad.

Cleaving means a unique loyalty between a man and woman that says, "Our home is a refuge against the world and the winds of change." Even in a dating relationship, you can develop a sense of commitment that, if the relationship results in marriage, will build to a sense of cleaving. From the beginning, you can begin a mental commitment even if it is just for that one date. It is all too easy to go out with someone and have wandering eyes all evening, focusing on everyone else who looks interesting. Instead, you can focus on that one person who is your date, thinking how you can be of help and encouragement to him or her just for that evening.

As your relationship grows increasingly serious, develop higher levels of commitment. When I became engaged to Paula, the question kept coming back to my mind over and over again, *In what ways can I commit myself to her for a lifetime? I have seen so many relationships disintegrate and fail. How can I develop a commitment to her that is not going to break apart over the years?*

Finally, I realized that God is the only one who knows the future as well as the present. If He is guiding me to marry Paula, then He is the one who will give me the ability to commit myself to her for the rest of my life. Christ committed Himself to us forever and He knows what commitment is all about. As I align myself with His heart, then He will give me the commitment that I desperately need.

The third aspect of marital unity is to be *one flesh*. This means that two individuals merge together into a single, unique unit. They don't lose their individuality. They are not submerged into the whole relationship. Rather, their individuality is enhanced by being a part of each other.

Some people interpret *one flesh* to be where a man is on his life's path and a woman comes along and hooks into the man's path. Others believe it is where there is a woman's path and the man comes over and hooks into hers. Still others define it as both keeping their individual paths which happen to meet on occasion.

None of these is correct. Rather, a unique woman and a unique man, on two different paths, come together to forge a third path. The merger is a new relationship, unique in every way, so that the third road is something totally new. Never before has this particular road been traveled. This new road helps fill out each of their personalities and characters. It is a lifelong path of discovery, enjoyment and adventure.

Obviously, the consummation of a lifetime commitment in marriage is sexual intercourse. Being of *one flesh* is represented not just by intercourse, however. That is a sign of it but unity is also the merging together of two people onto one road of life.

In dating we work in the social, emotional, mental and spiritual areas of life. The physical area is placed in God's hands to be the final consummation after the commitment of marriage has been made publicly before God and others.

The dating goal of unity is to be teachable regarding the other person. Learn how to build harmony by discovering how to enhance each other's personality and strengths and minimize the weaknesses. Discover where you are needed in the other person's life to strengthen weak areas and to complete the person.

Dating Goal 2: Being Spirit-filled

> And do not get drunk with wine, for that is dissipation, but be filled with the Spirit, speaking to one another in psalms and hymns and spiritual songs, singing and making melody with your heart to the Lord; always giving thanks for all things in the name of our Lord Jesus Christ to God, even the Father; and be subject to one another in the fear of Christ (Ephesians 5:18-21).

To be Spirit-filled is to have a daily dependence upon the Holy Spirit Himself. According to Scripture, the Spirit of God is the source of daily power of life, not just in a marriage, but in every aspect of our lives. If we are Christians, then the Holy Spirit is inside us. Activating the Spirit's power in us comes through believing that this is possible, and then becoming Spirit-reliant instead of self-reliant, not only in power but in the guidance for our lives.

I strongly recommend reading Bill Bright's *The Holy Spirit*[1] to learn how to be filled with the Holy Spirit by faith and to experience all the power, joy and overflow of God in your life that the Spirit is meant to bring.

The Spirit of God is to affect our speech, our behavior and our attitudes. A Spirit-filled attitude is one that gives thanks for all things, even when the going gets tough and the circumstances seem difficult. The Spirit-filled attitude also includes being subject to other Christians in the fear of Christ. That is, to realize that we are to be subject first to Him and second to each other. The key to a harmonious relationship is being humble, respecting each other's opinions and thoughts and honoring one another before the Lord.

When I told Paula that I loved her and wanted her to be my wife, I told her she would always be second in my life. Jesus Christ would be first. If Paula were to be first in my life, I could not personally generate the love that she should receive. Only as Christ energizes me and motivates me, providing His love for Paula through me, can she have all the love through me that she needs.

On the other hand, Paula does not put me first in her life. She gets her strength and fulfillment first from God Himself. Should either of us put the other first, then the other becomes that person's god. Jesus Christ must be God of all and overflow His love through each of us to the other through His Holy Spirit.

Through a Spirit-filled walk with Christ, we build toward maturity in relationships as He molds and develops our character. As we revere Jesus Christ we learn to be subject to or humble toward each other. When differences come into a relationship, we confront them not by arguing in a spirit of contentiousness, but by being humble, kind and gentle toward each other.

Dating Goal 3: Building Love

In the book of Ephesians, right after the apostle Paul admonished us to be filled with the Spirit of God, he begins to talk about the marriage relationship. He says that "husbands ought also to love their own wives as their own bodies. He who loves his own wife loves himself; for no one ever hated his own flesh, but nourishes and cherishes it, just as Christ also does the church, because we are members of His body.... This mystery is great; but I am speaking with reference to Christ and the church" (Ephesians 5:28-32).

In marriage, the man is commanded by God to love his wife with a love represented by the love Jesus had for the church — the people for whom He sacrificed Himself and died. For what reason did He do this? So that He could sanctify the church — set it apart and elevate it above all else. This is the same type of love that a husband ought to have for his wife. This kind of love must come, first of all, through submission to Jesus Christ.

It is my understanding of this passage that the man ultimately holds the responsibility of the home. He is to set the standard and be the guardian and protector of the home. When decisions are to be made, he consults with his wife and interacts with her on various possibilities. In the final analysis, however, he must make the decision and be accountable for it before God.

In dating, a man can learn to love consistently. He needs to learn that love is given not just when everything is fine and the emotions are flowing and romance is in the air. Love should flow even when moments are uninspiring, routine and dull, and even when there have been misunderstandings or periods of silence. Love seeks the highest and best for the other person. A man needs to become a student of the Scriptures — to find and follow God's path above all else — in order to develop these characteristics.

To develop the leadership abilities needed in marriage, he needs to learn to choose what is best for the relationship in order to give security to the woman. He needs to sacrifice his desires and idiosyncrasies for her sake.

In a dating relationship, however, a man should remember that he is not married to the woman. Therefore, he does not have to commit himself to her totally or sacrifice totally for her. At the same time, showing leadership does not mean to act like the lord and master or like he knows everything. Christ didn't do that even though he had the qualifications for it. A man doesn't have the qualifications. While exerting leadership, he must remember that men are to "be subject to one another in the fear of Christ" (Ephesians 5:21). That means to be humble, respect each other and have mutual harmony.

In a marriage relationship, "Wives, be subject to your own husband as to the Lord" (Ephesians 5:22) says that, as she has given herself to Christ, a wife should give herself to her husband.

She should understand that humility and direction are from Christ, not from her husband. Christ provided an environment where He accepted, sacrificed and gave to the church, and the church responded in love, understanding and subjection. Even so, the husband is to provide that kind of environment and atmosphere in which the wife can respond in gratitude and respect.

In such a home, there is equality of persons and yet a difference in function. Sexual barriers are broken down. The apostle Paul wrote, "There is neither Jew nor Greek, there is neither slave nor free man, there is neither male nor female; for you are all one in Christ Jesus" (Galatians 3:28). The woman is not greater than the man, nor the man greater than the woman.

In dating, and later in the home, the woman needs to respect the man and to respond to him as he tries to provide an atmosphere of love and acceptance. A woman cannot respond to a person she doesn't respect, so it is important to build that respect for him. Don't pull him down or pick him apart. Be careful not to be contentious but to encourage and build him up. It is important for a woman, as well as a man, to pick good material for a marriage partner.

After Paula and I were engaged, we went for pre-marital counseling with a Christian psychologist. After reviewing the personality tests he had given us, he made an interesting observation. He noticed that I am a very objective person. I see facts and figures and come up with logical conclusions. My score was the highest you can get in this regard, at the very top of the scale of objectivity. Paula's score, on the other hand, showed that she is far more subjective in her reasoning. Her score was in the normal range between subjectivity and objectivity. Then the psychologist made this statement, "Dick, when it comes to making decisions and seeing circumstances as they truly are, most of the time Paula will be right." That killed me! I did not want to believe that. Yet, after several years of marriage, I can say the statement is absolutely true. Much of the time Paula is right. I have learned to depend upon her wisdom and insights.

In dating, a woman should help to develop a harmonious spirit in the relationship. She can learn how to encourage a man and to point him to the Lord Jesus and the Scripture. As she dates, she can develop a spirit of cooperation toward her date regarding decisions they make as a couple.

If a woman feels put down or squelched, she may want to look for another man. She should feel free to discuss her thoughts openly and freely. She should be able to give her opinions without being looked down upon.

It is wonderful to me when Paula says over and over, "I believe in you, Dick. I know you can do it." Such words would not mean nearly as much if I didn't have confidence in her opinions and insight.

A woman should develop a confidence in God and experience His peace, that gentle and quiet spirit that comes from being filled with His Holy Spirit. We are all commanded to submit to one another. But the unique form of submission of a wife to a husband is found only in the marriage relationship. It doesn't refer to a woman who is dating a man. If a date doesn't provide for her an atmosphere of acceptance, commitment, wholesome morality and godliness, she should be skeptical. She should choose husband material, someone to whom she can easily submit, not just a romantic lover.

For Paula, the most helpful lesson she learned about submission to a husband was through a working relationship she had before we were married. She worked closely with the director of a campus ministry for Campus Crusade for Christ. Paula was the woman's coordinator in charge of the women's ministry on that campus. The director valued Paula's input, gave her responsibility for various activities, took her suggestions with a teachable spirit and worked together with her in close harmony. Paula loved her role, but she also loved the fact that she knew the final responsibility for everything they were doing lay with him. This gave her a great umbrella of freedom under which to work. At the same time, it took many burdens off her shoulders.

This is now the way that she and I work together in marriage. Paula helps me out tremendously. We divide up responsibilities and I love building her up as well. When the few times come that we disagree regarding a decision that has to be made, she gives me her input and then relaxes as I make the final decision. Why does she relax? Because she knows that ultimately I will have to answer to God for our decisions. The buck stops with me and she is home free. She views this as another way that God so wonderfully and masterfully designed ways to protect her.

Spiritual Guidelines for Dating

1. Commit your relationship to God.

Realize that the burden of your relationship is not on you but on God. He is the Creator, the Lord God of the universe, the one who has all things under His control. He knows your past, present and future, and He knows all about the person you are dating.

Too often we want to control everything ourselves. We like to feel as if we have the upper hand and that nothing is going to surprise us. But we are finite; the future is really a mystery to us.

The basis for a good relationship then is God's Word. His thoughts are on paper, there for you and me to see. Knowing His thoughts takes the pressure off us and puts it on Him. We should allow our expectations for a dating relationship to come from Him, not from our own romanticized desires.

Paula realized this after she broke up with a fellow she had been dating seriously. In reading the psalms, she saw the words, "My soul, wait in silence for God only, for my hope is from Him" (Psalm 62:5). She realized that she had been putting her expectations and hopes in marriage and not in the Lord Himself. In fact, she had been in love with the thought of being married, instead of being in love with the man.

2. Recognize open spaces and fences.

As we seek God's will, He will show us every twist and turn in the road and He knows where that road is going. When we trust a relationship to Him, He will guide us and give us room to grow and expand that relationship. But sometimes He also puts fences on a relationship and says, "Here are My limits." He pulls people apart because He knows that they are not best for each other. Not all love is meant to be marriage love. Even if we don't know why, God does.

In college, I was devastated when Amy told me she no longer wanted to date me. She was a strong Christian and I had thought we were headed toward marriage. Three years later, I was working with Campus Crusade for Christ at the University of Georgia. At

Christmas time, I went home to New Jersey to visit my parents. From a friend, I learned that Amy was in a nursing school in New York City, a twenty-minute drive away. On a whim, I gave her a call, and asked her if she would like to go out and talk about old times. She accepted.

That night, as we talked, I asked, "Do you still counsel women like you used to in college? So many women enjoyed talking with you then."

"Oh yes," she answered, "but I don't counsel like you do. You talk about Jesus Christ in your counseling, don't you?"

"Well, sure," I replied. "He's the only one who can meet people's needs."

"I don't believe that any more," she told me. "In fact, I don't believe in God any more. I have my boyfriend and he is all I really believe in now."

I was stunned. She continued to downgrade God amidst her swearing. In college when I was growing in my faith, she had been right there with me. I ended up strong for the Lord and wanting to serve Him. Unknown to me, she had gone the opposite way.

As I said good night that evening, I was very thankful to God that He had removed Amy from my life. Her inner character was so different from what I wanted in a wife. She had chosen a different path. God knew this three years previously and saved me from becoming further committed to her. How thankful I am that God built a fence in our relationship and stopped our progress toward marriage.

3. Expect prayer, not pressure, to build response.

Sometimes, when we really love a person, that person may not share the enthusiasm we have for our relationship. When this happens, we tend to manipulate and force the other person to respond to us. Such manipulative pressure usually has an undesired effect. It's more likely to make a person run away than draw closer to us. Pressure causes a person to feel boxed in and controlled. Spontaneity and a sense of fun are lost.

Sometimes, of course, pressure works for awhile. A person may even marry us under pressure. But when he or she realizes how much pressure was exerted to achieve this, respect will be lost. Instead of respecting our ability as a master manipulator, the other person will see that we are a master at selfishness, going after what we want, instead of desiring whatever is best for the other person.

Pressure confuses a person. The person who is being pushed along doesn't know if he or she really likes us or not. Eventually, it will cause doubt as to the commitment that has been made.

Manipulation shows that the manipulator is selfish, insecure and afraid of losing. Otherwise, the person would have been willing for the relationship to develop freely. Only in free response can a relationship be a lasting one.

When I started dating Paula, she lived in Tallahassee, Florida; I lived in San Bernardino, California. I was constantly traveling, speaking on campuses and at conferences, and had had previous long-distance relationships fail. But I had often tried to force a person to like me. I determined never to pressure Paula to write or phone me. I sent her many cards, but I never sent one that suggested, "My mailbox is lonely."

I tried not to put guilt on her. I simply prayed that God would motivate her heart. Once every nine or ten days, she would write. I would write back at her level but shorten the time slightly. I would send a letter in seven or eight days and then shorten it a little more the next time. But I never wanted her to write because of guilt complex.

I figured, if I can trust God's working in my heart and life, then I can trust Him to work in Paula's life, too. The writer of Proverbs hit the nail on the head. He said, "The king's heart is like channels of water in the hand of the Lord; He turns it wherever He wishes" (Proverbs 21:1). I thought, if God could turn a king's heart, He could turn a woman's heart to love me, if this is what He wanted. Why not pray that He would motivate Paula to like me? How much better to have spontaneous love and caring than to manipulate it. Let internal motivation from God be the source of pressure. Be a person of prayer seeking to have God's hand in the relationship.

4. Change obstacles into opportunities.

Every couple runs into obstacles in their relationship. It is the strong couple that will pray together about such problems, talk them out and search the Scriptures for God's answers. Some Christians over-spiritualize their search for answers to problems. They talk only to God about them but not to the other person. Others blame God for bringing differences up that are obviously human differences. They decide these differences are an automatic sign that God wants the relationship discontinued. They fail to see that obstacles are often opportunities for growth in the relationship. Working through obstacles is difficult, but continue with the relationship until God makes it plain that you shouldn't. Use these obstacles to develop your faith together and your commitment to one another.

In my book, *Faith — A 31-Day Experiment,*[2] I explain that faith has three ingredients: knowledge, affirmation and conviction. *Knowledge* refers to knowing God's Word and knowing God Himself. *Affirmation* is developing a positive response to the things you learn from God's Word. *Conviction* is taking that knowledge and positive response and putting it into practice.

When you come across the obstacles, differences or even annoying habits of your dating partner, instead of being frustrated or exploding over them, seek the Lord's guidance in these things. Use these obstacles to search the Scriptures, to develop stronger faith in Him and to find that He can carry you through them.

5. Develop spiritual harmony.

To develop together, spiritually, first develop a personal relationship with Christ. Have daily communion with Him, and be learning to abide in Him. In your dating, discover how each of you relates to God. You don't have to think exactly alike regarding all spiritual issues. However, you both need to have a dependence upon God to guide you individually and together.

The Bible is very clear that we should not be unequally yoked with unbelievers. That ought to apply not only to marriage, but to dating, since dating is the foundation for marriage. Those who are not Christians are self-reliant and not God-reliant. No matter how good they seem to be, their lives run contrary to God's will for your own life.

I come across many people who dated non-Christians, developed an emotional attachment and married them. Why do they do this? Often I hear the following reason: "I'm strong. I can handle this." Such reasoning can be likened to two people, one standing on a table and the other on the floor, each wanting to get the other to their own level. It's much easier for a person to pull you down to the floor than it is for you to pull the other person up on the table.

Another excuse offered is, "I'm praying that God will use me in this person's life." This is sometimes labeled "missionary dating." God may want to use you in that person's life but, on the other hand, He may not. It may be that Satan is wanting to use that person in your life, instead! When you date a non-Christian, you compromise your spiritual values for the relationship.

One person told me, "Well, I love him and God loves him, so he will change for me." Don't be fooled. Even if the person says that he or she will become a Christian, don't marry that person (or promise to marry) until the person asks Christ into his or her life, until that person exhibits spiritual change resulting from that decision and until he or she has had time to grow and settle in the faith. Too often a Christian marries a person who promised to become a Christian or who even showed initial signs of a conversion experience, only to live the rest of their lives with someone who does not serve or love Christ.

On the other hand, should your non-Christian dating partner become a "fired-up" Christian, and start studying the Scriptures, that person will want to know what you were doing dating him or her as a non-Christian! That person's Christian standards may end up being higher than yours in which case you are likely to break up anyway. You may have had a hand in that person becoming a Christian, but your refusal to date a non-Christian might have had as powerful an effect on the person's eventual conversion to Christ and left a greater respect for your Christian convictions. I've known this to happen in several instances.

A similar caution applies to a committed Christian dating a cold or lukewarm Christian where God is definitely not first in the person's life. Too often it is the committed Christian who changes, whose zeal for God dies down, whose eyes are turned away from God.

Ask yourself these questions regarding your dating partner:
- Does my dating partner bring out the best or the worst in me?
- Does that partner have a relationship with Christ that builds me up?
- Does he or she seek God's guidance in our relationship or depend upon self?
- Do I have to prop up this person spiritually or is he or she able to stand alone spiritually?

Spiritual Activities for Dating

Sharing spiritual activities with a dating partner will not only bring you closer together, but will keep your eyes on the Lord, the source of strength for making your relationship a godly one.

Minister to one another by taking part in one or more of the following activities. These are given in the order that you might want to consider them, depending on how long you have known or dated each other.

- Share your own spiritual thoughts and experiences, past and present.
- If you like to sing, put psalms to music, compose praise songs to the Lord or sing along with recorded Christian music.
- Relate your spiritual heritage, including your personal testimony of how you first met Christ.
- Discuss the content of sermons, books and tapes that you hear or read together.
- Take turns returning thanks before meals.
- Discuss doctrines of the faith. If you don't understand each other's beliefs, look for explanatory helps in a Christian bookstore or church library, or from a pastor or other theologically trained person.
- Exchange encouraging Scriptures each day.
- Memorize Scripture verses together and repeat them to one another.
- Do a regular Bible study together, perhaps using a Bible study book like *The 31-Day Experiment*[3] to keep you on track.
- Share personal spiritual battles and victories, past and present.
- Share each other's purposes in life and how each of you wants to glorify God.

- Write notes during personal Bible study and prayer times and later discuss these together.
- Pray together on a regular basis.

When praying together, I would caution you regarding hidden problems that might arise. Some couples struggle with sharing very personal feelings and intimate thoughts in prayer because it leads to a driving desire for deeper intimacy in emotional and physical areas. Perhaps choose a time for prayer together early in the evening, rather than late at night when physical tiredness may relax moral convictions.

During their engagement period, one couple I know phoned each other nightly before they turned in and prayed together on the telephone. In this way, they developed a spiritual intimacy and foundation for their marriage without this special intimacy leading toward temptations they couldn't control.

Reach out and minister to others together, as your relationship develops. Don't be exclusive in your relationship. Sometimes sharing about Christ and the Christian life together is easier than doing it on your own. Consider growing spiritually as a couple by taking part in some of the following activities with each other:

- Attend a regular Bible study.
- Lead a Bible study.
- Teach Sunday school.
- Visit people in the hospital or in retirement homes or other shut-ins.
- Participate in church visitation.
- Invite non-Christian couples to dinner and share Christ.
- Work with a youth group.
- Teach mutual skills or hobbies to others, sharing your faith whenever possible.
- Go on organized summer missions projects.
- Attend Christian growth or ministry training seminars.
- Counsel other couples.

Summary

Make it your practice and determination to seek the Lord, to love Him fully and to have a spiritual passion for Him when dating or not dating. Develop personal spiritual characteristics that will be good ground for a future marriage relationship. Bring that passion for Christ into your friendship where you and another person can seek the Lord and develop a true spiritual harmony.

Ask God to bring about togetherness through internal motivation. Don't try to force another person to like you.

Look for open spaces in a relationship where you can grow and build spiritual oneness together. But be aware of obstacles. Discern through prayer, interaction and the Scriptures whether these obstacles are opportunities for growth together or fences put up by God to lead you apart.

Make dating an experience of spiritual growth whether the relationship ends up being a prelude to marriage or a preparation for developing other star-balanced relationships in the abundant life God offers you.

1. What role does the spiritual aspect play in your relationships?

2. How can you develop this aspect in your relationships now?

3. What is your personal relationship with Christ?

Section Three

How to ~~Find~~ Become
The Right Person

Chapter Thirteen
Build Qualities That Attract

After dating many women, I came up with the general character traits of the woman I wanted. I called her my GOIA woman. Through experience, I had learned what I liked best. The things I was looking for were not items to check off on a list but overall character qualities. I began to pray for this woman even before I met her. I prayed that she would be:

G — Godly. She didn't have to be a super-spiritual giant, but I desired a woman who would have an independent, warm relationship with God. I knew that she would relate to God in different ways than I did but I just wanted a woman who had a strong, growing faith in Christ.

O — Outgoing. I tend to be on the quiet side, although some people find that hard to believe. On dates I enjoy listening. When I dated a quiet listener, silence reigned. I needed a woman who was more outgoing than myself, one who would make the conversation lively and draw me out.

I — Intelligent. Hopefully, the woman for me would enjoy conversing on a variety of topics. She didn't have to have a Ph.D., but I hoped she would want to expand her mind and mine, also.

A — Attractive. I wasn't looking for a cover girl knock-out. But I was looking for someone who was attractive to me. I didn't care what anyone else thought of her as long as I thought she was attractive.

Through the years of being single, I realized that it was all right to have *general* ideas of what you want in a mate. But don't keep a long list of specifics. Too many times someone has told me, "The person God gave me is so different from what I had anticipated." Don't get locked into a set of demands that drastically limit your choices.

As I looked for my GOIA woman, I was very aware that I needed to develop characteristics that would be attractive and personally fulfilling to her. A woman I was dating gave me an interesting thought. "When you get right down to it," she said, "it's not the outside that ultimately is important. It's the heart, personality and character." How wise she was. As Christian men and women, we need to build inner characteristics that are magnetic, that draw to us not just the other sex but people in general.

The Attractiveness of Spiritual Fruit

Attractive qualities originate in God. He is the most attractive of all. His character is filled with all that is perfect and beautiful. Because Christ is God, the qualities He displays shows the divine nature to us. One of the benefits of following Christ is that God is making us and molding us to become like Him. "And we know that God causes all things to work together for good to those who love God, to those who are called according to His purpose" (Romans 8:28).

The potential for God-likeness is unlimited. Due to the indwelling of the Holy Spirit, we can allow God, by faith, to produce in us all the beauty of the Father. Our motivation is to reflect His character to the world. "So that you may walk in a manner worthy of the Lord, to please Him in all respects, bearing fruit in every good work and increasing in the knowledge of God; strengthened with all power, according to His glorious might, for the attaining of all steadfastness and patience" (Colossians 1:10,11).

As a result of pleasing God, we will become attractive to others, especially to those who want to honor the Lord in their lives. We can study God's Word diligently and apply it in such a way as to develop the characteristics and behavior God wants for us. The amazing thing is that the Lord has not left us on our own to do the impossible. Rather, He has come to give us the desire and the power to do the possible. The apostle Paul acknowledged this when he wrote, "For it is God who is at work in you, both to will and to work for His good pleasure" (Philippians 2:13).

The Holy Spirit is the means by which God produces godly character in us. As a tree produces fruit after its kind, so God is producing His fruit in us so that we will become like Him in our character, attitudes and behavior.

"But the fruit of the Spirit is love, joy, peace, patience, kindness, goodness, faithfulness, gentleness, self-control" (Galatians 5:22,23). These are the characteristics the Spirit wants us to produce. Therefore, if we pray that the Lord will develop these traits in us and actively endeavor to mature in these areas, God will cause us to become the attractive persons He wants us to be.

As we focus attention on each fruit, remember that it is God's will and purpose for us to possess all of them. Don't be like Benjamin Franklin. He chose several admirable traits that he desired for his life. He worked on producing one each week. He was somewhat successful the first week on trait number one. As he was concentrating on the second trait the next week, however, his efforts to maintain the first trait failed. He couldn't succeed in more than one trait at a time. Frustrated and defeated, he gave up.

Don't give up. We have the Holy Spirit to produce and develop these attractive qualities in us. We are not left alone to depend upon ourselves. Daily trust Him to provide power in your life to exhibit these qualities.

Love

Much has been written on this subject and I have already discussed many aspects of love. But one area needs re-emphasizing. Learn to love yourself.

We are made in the image of God with unique strengths and weaknesses. Although the greatest commandment, Jesus said, was to love God with your whole being, the second one was to "love your neighbor as yourself" (Matthew 22:39). Love what God has made you.

A healthy self-esteem is a great gift to give someone. If you accept yourself, then you will be willing to accept your neighbor, your friends and your dating partner. Base your love not on circumstances or on fleeting feelings but on God's great love for you. He is the greatest example of genuine sacrificial love. As He has done for you, take every opportunity to do loving things for other people. Go out of your way to help meet people's needs even if they don't appreciate your efforts. Christ went to the cross to demonstrate His love for us. To what lengths will you go to express your love?

Joy

To delight in the Lord is to be filled with appreciation for all that He is: His power, holiness, justice, mercy, greatness and love. He is the object of joy and the more you learn about His attributes, the more your heart will be filled with gladness. The prophet Jeremiah exclaimed, "Thy words were found and I ate them, and Thy words became for me a joy and the delight of my heart" (Jeremiah 15:16). So daily feast upon the Scriptures and allow your heart to be flooded with gladness.

Look at the positive side of situations. There is nothing so dull and boring as listening to someone complain all the time. The apostle Paul could have had a defeated attitude about being in prison for four years. On the contrary, while in prison, he told the Philippian church, "Rejoice in the Lord always; again I will say, rejoice!" (Philippians 4:4).

How do you react when the pressures of life look like they will crush you? What reaction do you have in the midst of great disappointments? On the way to the cross, Christ had in His mind the "joy set before Him" (Hebrews 12:2). That was the door to salvation for all. Be encouraged. Praise the Lord always.

Peace

If there is anything we need, it is a calm mind and stomach in this fast- paced world. Whenever people were fretful in the Scriptures, God would say, "Do not tremble or be dismayed, for the Lord your God is with you wherever you go" (Joshua 1:9). Acknowledging the presence of God is the best antidote of all for anxious thoughts and situations.

Be willing to take risks in relationships, in developing the star of intimacy and in meeting new people. Let Christ's peace fill your mind (John 14:27).

Make prayer your constant attitude. Rest in the power of the Lord to work all things to His will. Become a peacemaker in relationships and endeavor to bring harmony between people. Others are attracted to someone who is calm in the midst of stormy circumstances. "Let the peace of Christ rule in your hearts" (Colossians 3:15).

Patience

I saw a cartoon showing a little girl kneeling beside her bed. "Dear Lord, I ask for patience, and I want it right now!"

Isn't that like us? We find it difficult to wait for anything. But God is not unnerved. He is totally in control. Nothing takes Him by surprise. He is always on time, never too late and never too early.

Be patient with people and circumstances. Ask God to give you His perspective on time. We need to develop the kind of endurance that a marathon runner has. Mile after mile he plods along, focusing his mind on the as yet unseen finish line. Allow the Holy Spirit to strengthen your endurance. Hope in God will never be misplaced.

If there are problems that have not been resolved, even after months or years, keep trusting God's power to work things out. If someone continually disturbs you, persevere under the pressure. If your job is boring or tedious, make the best of that day for God's glory and leave the future up to Him. "Those who wait for the Lord will gain new strength; they will mount up with wings like eagles, they will run and not get tired, they will walk and not become weary" (Isaiah 40:31).

Kindness

Isn't it interesting that God gives us commands in areas that are difficult, if not impossible, for us? When Christ talked about our attitudes and actions toward people who are antagonistic or apathetic toward us, He told us to be gracious toward them.

"But love your enemies, and do good, and lend, expecting nothing in return; and your reward will be great, and you will be sons of the Most High; for He Himself is kind to ungrateful and evil men" (Luke 6:35). Don't let your tongue tear people apart or put people down. Be gracious in your speech and actions.

Cultivate hospitality. Invite people for dinner and try your skills at cooking. Be open-hearted to new people who attend your group meetings. Make someone else's day by being loving and pleasant, even if they have been obnoxious or withdrawn.

Goodness

Pick up any newspaper or news magazine and you will read about how wickedly and selfishly people treat one another. Our world is full of wars, terrorism, strife and destruction. In a similar situation, the psalmist said, "I would have despaired unless I had believed that I would see the goodness of the Lord in the land of the living" (Psalm 27:13). In a darkened world of sin, God's goodness shines like a thousand suns. The word *good* refers to moral integrity and righteous character. Let God's character shine through you. When the person you are dating wants to step across God's moral boundary, take a stand on the side of purity. Be ethical and above reproach in all your dealings with people. God is a just God and wants us to be honorable in everything.

Paul admonishes us, "Instruct them to do good, to be rich in good works, to be generous and ready to share, storing up for themselves the treasure of a good foundation for the future, so that they may take hold of that which is life indeed" (1 Timothy 6:18,19).

Faithfulness

To be trustworthy is a lost value in our society. People are out to get themselves ahead. It is hard to find someone who will keep his word and do what he says he will do. It is a rare individual who sticks with a friend through all contrary circumstances, even those which call for personal sacrifice.

But God is faithful. He is unwavering in His commitment to us, even when we fail Him. "If we are faithless, He remains faithful; for He cannot deny Himself" (2 Timothy 2:13). His trustworthiness always is steady in uncertain times.

Through the power of the Holy Spirit, become a person of your word. If you commit yourself to something, carry through your promise without excuses, or negligence or quitting. Show people that you can be counted on by doing quality work. Don't cut corners or sluff off. If you do prove undependable, humble yourself and admit your mistakes. Don't rationalize your sins. People will see right through dishonesty. If you are a fake, others will never trust you. Be genuine and earn their confidence in you.

Gentleness

In a world where power means to step on people, tenderness is considered weakness — a characteristic of losers. But look at the way Christ treated people. Rome was in power and ruled the world with an iron fist at that time, but Rome was destroyed long ago. Christ's sensitive love still draws people to the cross today. That is one reason I responded to Him.

Have you ever watched parents hold a newborn baby? They are gentle, considerate, helpful, loving and tender. The apostle Paul said that this was the way he treated people: "But we proved to be gentle among you, as a nursing mother tenderly cares for her own children. Having thus a fond affection for you, we were well pleased to impart to you not only the gospel of God but also our own lives, because you had become very dear to us" (1 Thessalonians 2:7,8). But Paul also exhorted, encouraged and implored each one of them as a father would his own children so that they would live a life pleasing to the Lord (1 Thessalonians 2:10-12). Gentleness is not only being tender but being strong for what is right. Correct someone in a gentle manner, not harshly or with a revengeful heart.

Develop a forgiving attitude toward people who have wronged you. Let the Lord cleanse your mind of any bitterness you may harbor. Learn to comfort other hurting people with the same comfort you have received from the Lord.

Self-Control

Our imaginations love to run wild. Our appetites crave all kinds of foods that are not good for us. We enjoy being lazy and spreading rumors about people. Jealousy can grab us in an instant and a sharp tongue can easily get us into trouble. In countless ways, we see attitudes in ourselves that are not pleasing to God. Temptations constantly hit us in our weak spots.

How can we handle all these powerful attitudes and emotions? Without God we are uncontrollable. But that is just the point, for self-control is really Spirit-control. Only He can channel our energies and tame our wildness. He doesn't stifle us or put us in a strait jacket. Ironically, when He controls us, we are set free.

To become disciples in the Lord is to place ourselves under His authority and to be closely yoked to Him. His power is available to set us free from anything that binds or enslaves us. He can break the chains of bad habits or addictions to ungodly practices.

Discipline is an ugly word in our society today, but it is the key word for being a disciple. Obedience to Christ shows our deep love for Him. Self-control shows our loyalty to His will. We must learn to deal with the emotions and habits that pull us down. Keep coming to Him for direction and strength. Establish a daily devotional time of Bible study and prayer. Develop the art of stopping and thinking before reacting negatively to circumstances. Control your temper with the gentleness of Christ.

Paul understood all this. "Do you not know that those who run in a race all run, but only one receives the prize? Run in such a way that you may win.... Therefore I run in such a way, as not without aim; I box in such a way, as not beating the air; but I buffet my body and make it my slave, lest possibly, after I have preached to others, I myself should be disqualified" (1 Corinthians 9:24,26,27).

All these qualities are produced by abiding in the vine of Christ (John 15:5). Fruit grows when it is intimately connected with the source of life. If we receive our spiritual life from the Holy Spirit, we will develop all these traits.

One caution. Don't expect overnight results. Some areas may be easy for you; others may be difficult. But none is impossible. Producing fruit is a process that takes time. Don't get discouraged with temporary setbacks. Keep moving ahead with faith and confidence.

The Attractiveness of Praise

My favorite passage throughout my single years was Psalm 34. It begins, "I will bless the Lord at all times, except when I'm single." Think again. That's not the way it goes.

> I will bless the Lord *at all times*;
> His praise shall continually be in my mouth.
> My soul shall make its boast in the Lord;
> The humble shall hear it and rejoice.
> O magnify the Lord with me,
> And let us exalt the Lord together (Psalm 34:1-3).

The solution to living through the ups and downs of our lives is to praise the Lord. Why? Because we can praise God all the time. "I will bless the Lord at all times." There is no clause that adds, "except in certain disappointing situations."

When David wrote this psalm he was in a tight situation where he could have been killed (1 Samuel 21:10-15). He faked insanity so that everyone would leave him alone. He was left in the wilderness to wander as a crazed man. In the midst of this ordeal, he said, "I will praise the Lord continually." Why? Because God Almighty was still on His throne. He still knew how to work things out. Nothing takes God by surprise or defeats Him.

We know that God loves us and knows what is best for us at all times. Even when we are in the pit of despondency, God knows how to transform our lives. He knows how to raise us up and to put a new smile on our faces.

David said that we should praise the Lord on our own. Verse two of Psalm 34 reads, "My soul shall make its boast in the Lord." My soul — me — I'm proud of my God and I'll show it. The beginning of understanding how to trust God is hooking up with God and being assured that He is there to help you and to give you courage. Jesus Christ says the "mouth speaks from that which fills [the] heart" (Luke 6:45). The source of joy is to fill your life with the Lord and to get your heart right with Him. Then let the blessing and praise overflow.

David also exhorted us to praise Him not only on our own but with other people. "O magnify the Lord with me, and let us exalt His name together" (Psalm 34:3).

The closer you walk with God, the more refreshing, exhilarating and exciting life becomes. Other people want to get in on the action of trusting God and exalting Him. As He overflows your heart, others will want to enjoy the Lord with you and bless His name in a relationship of oneness.

Wrong Goals

Singles sometimes have wrong goals. One of these is pursuing marriage. We devise a blueprint for getting married. We build what I call air castles in the sky, saying, "Now, I just met so-and-so at work today. If I just happen to be in the right place at the right time, maybe he will notice me and we'll eventually get together." Or you remember someone you once dated, perhaps your first love, and you dream of getting back with that person.

The problem with living in such a fantasy world is that when you come back to reality you are frustrated. The more you build air castles, the more frustrated you become; you think you have to get married in order to be as happy as you were when dreaming.

Another wrong goal is trying to find the right person. Whenever you meet someone, you immediately ask yourself, "Is this the one? Let's see, I have my list of requirements for a mate right here. This person checks out on numbers one, two and three. But four and five, no. This person doesn't measure up here. Sorry."

The frustration is that no one will ever measure up to your list completely. The list adds tremendous pressure to finding the right one. It's hard to relax when meeting someone if the list is there in the forefront of your mind.

Right Goals

What does the Lord think about this? Instead of pursuing marriage, pursue the Lord. "I sought the Lord, and He answered me, and delivered me from all my fears: (Psalm 34:4). It is exciting to pursue the Lord. When you trust Him, the pain of not having someone that you pursued for marriage begins to be taken away. He delivers you from the fear of never getting married as well as from other fears.

God's viewpoint is to pursue love, not marriage. He has given us the single years to learn how to love faithfully, to learn how to give ourselves to someone else in friendship, to learn how to be the right person, to learn how to walk with the Lord, to learn how to be sensitive to another person's needs, to know what another person feels and to understand how to open our hearts to others.

People tell me that they are looking for a mate who can really help them walk with God and be their security. But if you need someone else to help you know God intimately, you have problems. Your walk with God is supposed to be a direct personal relationship with Him. It is not to be a vicarious, secondhand relationship through a mate or friend. Someone of the other sex who meets your specifications for godliness is not going to want you if you are a spiritual clinging vine or flat tire that needs to be pumped up. Each of us is responsible for our own walk with the Lord.

The right goal for singles is to become the right person. If you seek to be the right person, God will take care of finding the right mate for you.

The Single Adventure

If someone had told me in high school that I would have to wait so long to get married, I would have committed suicide. I wouldn't have known how to handle that thought.

What I have learned since then, however, is that life is a daily adventure with the Lord, married or single. Each day, a step at a time, we need to walk with Him in faithfulness, in trusting and in surrender. When we commit our way to Him, He guides our steps. We have a great God. He is infinitely creative and will meet you in your deepest needs and give you a quality of life that is straight from Him. The single life can be an exciting one that attracts other people to you, but only when you trust yourself to the Lord of your present and future life.

1. What inner characteristics do you think are important for you to develop?

2. What qualities in a person of the other sex are attractive to you?

3. How do you plan to develop the fruit of the Holy Spirit in your life?

Chapter Fourteen
Keep on the Right Path to the Right One

It had been a long six-month trip through twenty-two countries throughout Africa, Asia and the Middle East. I had been assisting the international staff of Campus Crusade for Christ in their ministries. Finally, I traveled back to the Philippines, my final stop before heading across the Atlantic toward home. I was twenty-eight years old, tired and lonely, and hadn't had a date the entire time.

Around dusk, I was walking through the art district of Manila toward my motel. Suddenly, before I realized what was happening, a gorgeous woman stepped out from between two buildings and walked toward me. She grabbed my hand and said, "Hi, how are you tonight?" I was taken completely off guard. "I'd like to give you a good time," she said. "Why don't we go to my apartment and have some fun?" I had always thought that prostitutes who walked the streets would be ugly, but this one was gorgeous, more so perhaps since I had not held a woman's hand for many months.

A battle raged within me. I would have loved just to be cared for and to feel a woman's warmth, yet the thought also hammered in my mind, *This is dangerous. Don't play with fire!*

She saw my hesitation and said, "Come on. My husband is on a long trip. He won't be back for weeks."

"No, I can't," were the only words that I could get out of my mouth. I was still overcome with struggle.

"Let's go," she said. "I know how to give you a really good time."

"No, I can't," I replied again. But in my heart I knew I was wavering. I knew that the desire for a woman was very strong.

Standing on the sidewalk, as I still struggled in my mind, the woman said, "Here's a taxi. Let's go. It will be a good time."

Weakly, I replied, "No, I can't."

Finally, she stopped pulling on my arm and said, "Why?" That little hesitation on her part gave me greater courage to say what was really on my mind. Even though I wanted that warmth and wanted someone to reach out to me, I knew it was wrong. Even though no one in the whole world would know that I had been with a prostitute, I would know and my God would know. And the memory would burn like acid in my soul.

"Because I believe in Jesus Christ," I blurted out.

She dropped my hand and looked at me, horror written in her eyes. "Are you a priest?" she asked.

"No, I am not!" Then with all the courage that I could muster, I started to speak loudly. "I believe in Jesus Christ! I am a Christian! My God is real and this is wrong! He is the Holy God above!" She became so frightened and angry that she turned and ran away.

I quickly went back to my motel room, shaken to the core of my being that I had come so close. I dropped to my knees and wept uncontrollably before God. The temptation had been so strong to get into the taxi with that woman. To think I had toyed around with fire and had almost been burned. Over and over again I cried, "Thank You God for Your strength! There is such power in the name, just saying the name of Jesus Christ! Thank You, Lord, that You gave me the courage to resist. You protected me! I have no one else to depend upon but You and You will never fail me."

The Lonely Places

For the next fourteen years I continued to be single. Everyone has struggles in life. As a single man, I had my own particular set. I felt the pain of loneliness often. Oh, yes, I had roommates and lots of friends, but I struggled with not having a woman to share my life. These feelings cropped up in a number of different situations.

One was in airports. Whenever I would get off a plane, there would be a crowd of people there to greet the arriving passengers. There would be lots of hugging and kissing. Little children would run up and yell, "Mommy, Daddy." But I had to walk through the middle of that crowd of happy people alone.

Another place where I had a hard time was in motel rooms. I was constantly traveling. Besides my overseas trips in my twenties, I began speaking and teaching in my thirties. The hardest thing for me was to speak to hundreds of people during my lectures and then to go back to my motel room by myself. The deafening silence of those four walls would close in on me. It was painful to be the only occupant of that room.

The other place that I struggled emotionally was at church. The whole church seemed to be filled with happy, smiling families. Parents would drop their kids off for Sunday School and then attend church. Afterward they would all get together and talk about their upcoming plans to spend Sunday afternoon together. Once again, it would hit me, *I don't have a family.*

Traveling itself produced a fight within me. So often on my trips, I would see marvelous scenery or witness the amazing power of God in people's lives as they responded to the talks I gave. I wanted to share that beauty and the feelings it produced in the depths of my soul, but there was no one. I could always tell the people with whom I associated in the many places I visited, but at each place the people were different. With no one person to share the deep thoughts and beauty of life, I felt robbed of companionship.

The Frustration of Jokes and Formulas

Loneliness wasn't my only struggle. People and their comments were, too. Some would talk about my single state jokingly but their words were like daggers in my heart.

"Why isn't a nice guy like you married?"

"Are you afraid to take responsibility?"

"Maybe you're just too picky. Maybe you should stop looking for just the perfect one."

"Aren't you really interested in women?"

"What are you waiting for?"

Other people, former single adults, would enthusiastically give me their advice. But one person's formula may be another person's frustration. They would say:

"When I finally gave up everything to God, then, very quickly afterward, God brought the right one along."

"Right after I learned a big lesson God wanted to teach me, He brought me my mate."

"When I stopped looking, then the Lord brought the person to me."

"When I finally came to grips with my singleness and said, 'Yes, I am willing to be single for the rest of my life,' then God brought the right one along."

These formulas may be good for some people, but, when I tried them, they didn't work. I had sincerely given my life to God when I was in college. I had served Him on the staff of Campus Crusade for Christ for more than eighteen years. I had been a pastor for four years. What did these people who married in their twenties know about singleness that I didn't know? But I continued to find no one with whom I wanted to build a home. I dated lots of women, but no one was special to me. Those formulas were not the answer.

The Right Path

I had my ups and downs as a single person. But I discovered that certain things kept me on the right path.

The first was the *Word of God*. It gave me a strong foundation for my life. I learned to stand on the truth, no matter what my feelings were or what circumstances confronted me. The Lord Jesus had called me to obey. "If anyone loves Me, he will keep My word. . ." (John 14:23). I couldn't go wrong trying to follow God's command to live a righteous life. The Scriptures became my guidebook for living.

The second was *God Himself.* Relating to the Lord was a source of joy and comfort. Prayer became for me a conversation with the God I loved. The rest of John 14:23 says, ". . .and My Father will love him, and We will come to him, and make Our abode with him." Openly and honestly, I learned to tell Him all my thoughts and feelings. He was the only lover I had and I poured out my soul to Him. I developed a committed spirit toward the Lord to follow Him no matter what it cost me. I made a lot of mistakes, but I found through the struggles a certain sense of confidence in Him; I knew He would never leave me or forsake me (Hebrews 13:5).

The third thing was *friends.* Friendship gave me caring companions. They became my "family." Whenever I traveled, I made friends and spent my spare time with them. When I came home, my roommates and the men in my CELL group that I talked about earlier encouraged me greatly.

The fourth was a *ministry.* There is nothing more fulfilling than meeting the needs of other people. The goal of my life was not to get married or to establish a home. It was to glorify God with my talents. My overriding desire was to give my energy to help people grow in Christ. Getting involved in the lives of others shifted my focus off myself and on to others.

The last was *interesting activities.* These expand a person's mind and make life fun. Being single provided me with the time to become involved in a variety of hobbies and sports.

With all of these, of course, there were still the "why" questions that I couldn't answer. Why did my older brother Herb get married at twenty-four and my younger brother Bob at twenty-five? How about me, Lord?

The Why of Singlehood

When I turned forty-one, I still did not have a wife or even a viable prospect. Some good female friends were in their thirties and unmarried. They were true GOIA (godly, outgoing, intelligent, attractive) women who loved Christ. Why weren't they married? Other friends got married in their early to mid twenties. Why do some get married and others not? I had no answers for these burning questions. But I turned to God's Word for His direction again and again.

I clung to a promise in Psalm 37:3-5. "Trust in the Lord, and do good; dwell in the land and cultivate faithfulness. Delight yourself in the Lord; and He will give you the desires of your heart. Commit your way to the Lord, trust also in Him, and He will do it."

This promise of God kept me strong in Him. I did not know when or how He would answer. It was His choice. My responsibility was to do good, to trust Him and to be faithful. I knew that He always wanted the best for me.

Finally, in the forty-first autumn of my life, I felt I was building a relationship with a woman who might possibly be the one. Paula invited me to her house for Thanksgiving. However, after two days, I felt discouraged. Our relationship was on rocky ground.

The following morning, I was sitting by a window in my motel room reading the Scriptures and asking God why things were falling apart just when I thought I had finally found a woman that I could really love. As I pored over the Scriptures in my anxiety, I came across the book of the prophet Habakkuk. Everything had gone wrong during his time and it looked as if his whole nation would be utterly destroyed by an invading army. But he turned in faith to God and said,

> "Though the fig tree should not blossom,
>   and there be no fruit on the vines,
> though the yield of the olive should fail,
>   and the fields produce no food,
> though the flock should be cut off from the fold,
>   and there be no cattle in the stalls,
> yet I will exult in the Lord,
>   I will rejoice in the God of my salvation.
> The Lord God is my strength,
>   and He has made my feet like hinds' feet,
> and makes me walk on my high places" (Habakkuk 3:17-19).

In my tears and bewilderment I cried out to God, "Oh Lord, even if Paula would never love me and I would remain single all the rest of my life, I submit my heart to You. Christ is my God and He is in control."

Later on that day, as Paula and I talked, I realized that I had been mistaken about her actions and intentions. Even though it all had been a misunderstanding, God had used this to clarify my motives. Whether or not He ever gave me a wife, I had reaffirmed my total commitment to Him.

Much to my delight and surprise, Paula and I became engaged about two months later. During the next four months leading up to our marriage, I pondered the question, "Why did God wait so long to give me a wife?" I didn't have an answer. I was still bewildered.

On our honeymoon, while relaxing on the beach one day, I looked off across the ocean contemplating this question. Paula interrupted my thoughts and said, "What are you thinking about?"

"Oh, nothing," I replied.

"Now, come on really, what are you thinking about?" she asked.

"Paula," I said, "for months I have struggled with the question, Why has God waited all these years to finally give me a wife?"

Without a moment's hesitation, she said, "I know!"

Flabbergasted, I replied, "You know?"

"Sure," she said, "if God had brought you someone sooner, it wouldn't have been me!"

That was a simple and yet profound answer. God knows the whys for each of us and He is sovereign. For me, He had been preparing the right woman and the right time all along.

References

Chapter 1 - The Search for a Lasting Love

1. C. S. Lewis, *Four Loves* (New York: Harcourt Brace Jovanovich, Inc., 1960), pp.11-12.
2. Josh McDowell, *His Image...My Image* (San Bernardino: Here's Life Publishers, 1984), p.110.

Chapter 2 - The Foundation for Love

1. Alan Loy McGinnis, *The Friendship Factor* (Minneapolis: Augsburg Publishing House, 1979), p.9.
2. Stuart Rosenthal, "The Need For Friendship in Marriage," *Medical Aspects of Human Sexuality* (November 1984), p.113.
3. David Smith, *The Friendless American Male* (Ventura: Regal Books, 1978), p.161.

Chapter 3 - Protect Your Heart

1. Marshall Hodge, *Your Fear Of Love* (Garden City: Doubleday, 1967), p.4.
2. Hugo Black, *Friendship* (Old Tappan: Fleming H. Revell Co., 1898), p.91.
3. Gabrielle Brown, *The New Celibacy* (New York: McGraw-Hill Book Company, 1980), p.73.
4. John Powell, *Why Am I Afraid To Tell You Who I Am?* (Niles: Argus Communications, 1969), p.12.
5. Dick Purnell, *31-Day Experiment* (San Bernardino: Here's Life Publishers, 1984).

Chapter 4 - Press for Instant Intimacy

1. Henry Brandt, "Must I Give Up Sex?" *Collegiate Challenge*, n.d., p.4.
2. Joyce Brothers, "A New Morality," *Time* (November 21, 1977).
3. Gabrielle Brown, *The New Celibacy* (New York: McGraw-Hill Book Company, 1980), p.17.

4. Elisabeth Haich, *Sexual Energy and Yoga* (New York: ASI Publishers, 1975), p.52.
5. Josh McDowell and Paul Lewis, *Givers, Takers and Other Kinds of Lovers* (Wheaton: Tyndale House Publishers, Inc., 1980), p.35.

Chapter 5 - Say Yes and Be Sorry

1. Jimmy Williams, *Why Wait Til Marriage?* (Dallas: Probe Books, 1979), p.11.
2. "Second Thoughts on Being Single," N.B.C. documentary, May 1984.
3. Jimmy Williams, *Why Wait Til Marriage?*, p.10.
4. Jerry Evans, "Sex Before Marriage — Why Should We Wait?" *His* (May 1981), p.4.
5. John Leo, "The Revolution Is Over," *Time* (April 9, 1984), p.83.
6. Carin Rubenstein, "The Modern Art of Courtly Love," *Psychology Today* (July 1983), p.44.
7. Robert O. Blood, Jr., *Marriage*, 2d. ed. (New York: Free Press), quoted in *Family Life* (October 1972), p.2.
8. Jerry Evans, "Sex Before Marriage," p.4.
9. E. Mansell Pattison, "Living Together: A Poor Substitute for Marriage," *Medical Aspects of Human Sexuality* (November 1982), pp.71-78.
10. R. J. Klein et al., "Herpes Simplex Virus Infections: An Update," *Hospital Medicine* (November 1983), p.170.
11. George Lewis, "Incidence of Asymptomatic Gonorrhea," *Medical Aspects of Human Sexuality* (October 1983), p.250.
12. Atlanta Center For Disease Control, Statistics Department (per phone conversation, 9/85).
13. "Chlamydia trachomatis common among sexually active adolescent women," Sexually Transmitted Disease Bulletin (October 1983). (See also: *Pediatrics*, March 1983, p.333ff.)
14. Interview with Masood A. Khatamee, "Chlamydia mycoplasm: What are the hidden risks of these STDs?" *Modern Medicine* (February 1984), p.156.

15. International Medical News Service: Chicago, "One Million Americans Treated for PID Each Year," *Family Practice News* (December 1-14, 1983), p.50.
16. Roundtable: "Consequences of Gonococcal Pelvic Inflammatory Disease," *Medical Aspects of Human Sexuality* (November 1983), p.105.
17. Julia Kagan, "Sexual Freedom: The Medical Price Women Are Paying," *McCall's* (May 1980), p.98.
18. International News Services: Gulf Shores, "Sees Cervical Cancer Epidemic With Current Life-styles," *Family Practice News* (August 1-14, 1984), p.3.
19. Nathan Horowitz, "Point to Cervical Cancer as Sexually Transmitted Disease," *Medical Tribune* (June 15, 1983), pp.3,9.
20. Nathan Horowitz, "Point to Cervical Cancer," p.9.
21. Felicia Lee, "Tubal Pregnancies Now Epidemic," *USA Today* (March 7, 1985), p.1-D.
22. Nathan Horowitz, "Ectopic Pregnancies Up, Now A Major Death Risk," *Medical Tribune* (January 26, 1983), p.3.
23. International Medical News Service: Washington, "Ectopic Pregnancy Rate Up but Errors In Its Dx Are Down," *Family Practice News* (December 15-31, 1983).
24. International Medical News Service: San Francisco, "Rate of Ectopic Pregnancy Has Doubled in U.S.," *Family Practice News* (January 15-31, 1983).
25. Jon R. Snyder, "Defusing the Deadly Ectopic," *Emergency Medicine* (November 30, 1983), p.92.
26. Michael Heller, "Generally Unrecognized Effects of Sexually Transmitted Diseases," *Medical Aspects of Human Sexuality* (January 1985), p.179.
27. Michael Heller, "Generally Unrecognized Effects," pp.186-93.
28. Michael Heller, "Generally Unrecognized Effects," p.193.
29. J. D. Unwin, *Sexual Regulations and Cultural Behavior*, copyright 1969 by Frank M. Darrow, P.O. Box 305, Trona, CA 93562.
30. Reo Christenson, "Prof Tells What Teens Need to Know Beyond Physiology of Sex," *Youth Letter* (November 1980).
31. James Dobson, *Emotions: Can You Trust Them?* (Ventura: Gospel Light Publications, 1980), p.65.

32. Richard Meier, Lorraine Meier, Frank Minirth and Paul Meier, *Sex in the Christian Marriage* (Richardson, TX: Today Publishers, Inc., 1985), p.141.

Chapter 6 - Expect Only Time To Heal

1. David Seamands, *Healing For Damaged Emotions* (Wheaton: Victor Books, 1981), p.96.
2. David Seamands, *Healing For Damaged Emotions*, p.99.
3. Chuck Swindoll, *Starting Over* (Portland: Multnomah Press, 1977), p.9.
4. Joan Jacobs, *Feelings, Where They Come From And How To Handle Them* (Wheaton: Tyndale House Publishers, 1976), p.22.
5. Lewis Smedes, *Forgive and Forget — Healing the Hurts We Don't Deserve* (San Francisco: Harper & Row, Publishers, 1984), pp.56,79.
6. Lewis Smedes, *Forgive and Forget*, p.39.
7. Erwin Lutzer, "How Much Can God Forgive?" *Kindred Spirit* (Winter 1977), p.6.
8. David Seamands, *Healing For Damaged Emotions*, pp.138-39.
9. C. S. Lewis, *The Screwtape Letters* (West Chicago: Lord and King Associates, Inc., 1976), pp.66-67,76,130.

Chapter 7 - Share Total Intimacy

1. Carl Rubenstein, *In Search of Intimacy* (New York: Delacorte Press, 1982), p.21.
2. Eugenia Price, *Make Love Your Aim* (Grand Rapids: Zondervan Publishing House, 1967), pp.25,59-60.

Chapter 9 - Have A Meeting Of Your Minds

1. Josh McDowell, *His Image...My Image* (San Bernardino: Here's Life Publishers, 1984), p.43.

Chapter 11 - Express Love Creatively

1. John Delameter, "The Social Control of Sexuality," *Annual Review of Sociology*, Vol. 7 (1981), p.272.

Chapter 12 - Explore Your Souls

1. Bill Bright, *The Holy Spirit* (San Bernardino: Here's Life Publishers, 1980).
2. Dick Purnell, *Faith: A 31-Day Experiment* (San Bernardino: Here's Life Publishers, 1985).
3. Dick Purnell, *The 31-Day Experiment* (San Bernardino: Here's Life Publishers, 1984).

You can keep in touch with Dick!

My staff team and I would like to thank you for your interest in part of God's work through the Dick Purnell Ministry. Prayer is vital to an ongoing ministry and we'd like you to be a part of our ministry by praying for us. Of course, in order for you to pray specifically for us, we would like to keep you up to date on our ministry activities.

Time-Out With Dick Purnell is a publication which will pass along interesting articles and news that will minister to your personal and spiritual needs. Our aim is to keep you informed of Dick's speaking events and other ministry news as well as letting you know our ministry needs.

I hope you will keep in touch with us by mailing in this coupon to receive your free subscription to **Time-Out With Dick Purnell**. We will look forward to hearing from you.

In His Joy,

Dick

Dick